SLINGSHOT

RE-IMAGINE YOUR BUSINESS, RE-IMAGINE YOUR LIFE

Gabor George Burt

Slingshot: Re-Imagine Your Business, Re-Imagine Your Life

Published by Franklin Green Publishing
500 Wilson Pike Circle, Suite 100
Brentwood, Tennessee 37027

www.franklingreenpublishing.com

Cover and book design by Bill Kersey, KerseyGraphics

Special thanks to Westley Overcash for his tireless contributions

Photographs and Illustrations
Special thanks to the students of St. Stephen School, Grand Rapids, Michigan for the
children illustrations, and Jason & John Waltrip for the Team-O graphics (2, 208, 210, 213).
The slingshot image used throughout the book, as well as photos on viii, 30, 53, 105, 152,
218 were created by the author.
Banksy: 172
iStockphoto: x, 84, 85
Look and Learn: 70, 147
News Channel 8, Tampa, FL: 10
Wikimedia Commons [CC-BY-SA-2.0 (www.creativecommons.org/licenses/by-sa/2.0)]
    BDriscoll [Public domain]: 39
    Ignaz_Semmelweis_1830 by Lénart Landau (1790-1868) [Public domain]: 66
    Koenigsegg_side by Ergonomidesign (Own work) [GFDL (http://www.gnu.org/
        copyleft/fdl.html)]: 181
    KUKA_Robocoaster_Robot_Arm by Andrew Skudder from UK (Robot): 32
    Nano_Tata by oval_BURNS: 187
    Rainforest_Cow_-_geograph.org.uk_-_182211 by Lisa Jarvis: 171
Wikimedia Commons [CC-BY-SA-3.0 (www.creativecommons.org/licenses/by-sa/3.0)]
    Flip_UltraHD_03_500 by Parkrocker.com (Own work): 34
    TransMilenio_Portal_Suba by Josegacel29 (Own work) [GFDL (http://www.gnu.org/
        copyleft/fdl.html)]: 107

Library of Congress Cataloging-in-Publication Data

ISBN 978-1-936487-073

Printed in the United States of America

1 2 3 4 5 6 7 8 9 10—15 14 13 12 11

To my professor and mentor,
W. Chan Kim, co-creator of Blue Ocean Strategy

"Adults are just obsolete children."
—Dr. Seuss, American author and illustrator (1904–91)

What if you could reclaim your childhood creativity
and sense of limitless possibilities

to overstep perceived limitations

for continuous business and personal success?

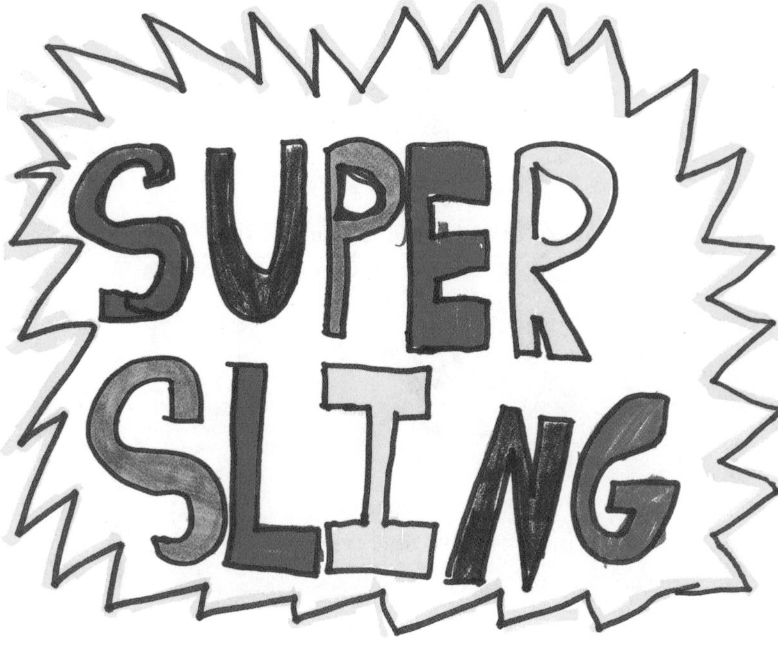
SUPER
SLING

CONTENTS

HOW TO IMMERSE YOURSELF IN *SLINGSHOT*

What you are about to read is no ordinary book. It is the centerpiece of a multisensory experience, supported by the book's website, **www.slingshotliving.com**. Here is how you can take advantage of each dimension:

1 **Enjoy the Illustrations:** The original artwork throughout the book was created by children from St. Stephen School in Grand Rapids, Michigan. Artists range from first to sixth grade and provide wonderful examples of the abundant creativity that children possess. When you come to an illustration, see if you can guess the age of the artist. Then visit the website and find the artist's answers to such important questions as:

- What would you like to be when you grow up?
- What do you think of grown-ups?
- Complete the question: What if…?
- What question do you have about why something works the way it does, and how could it work even better?

2 Listen to Slingshot Music: If you feel sufficiently adventurous, read *Slingshot* to our musical accompaniment. The enchanting original music is designed to guide your journey through the book and enhance your enjoyment. You can access the music via the website and listen to the songs in step with your progress through the book.

3 Talk and Discover: Perhaps you have immediate feedback and thoughts to share on something you read in the book. Or you want to contribute an idea or a work of art inspired by it. Then join the conversation and the artistic expressions on the website, and see what various experts, thought leaders, and pertinent media, as well as inventive adults and children, are up to.

4 Play: How better to recover the sensation of launching a toy slingshot than by holding the real thing? Visit the website and get one to play with—as you're reading.

5 Learn: Look for upcoming forums, both online and live, to learn more about the topics covered.

INTRODUCTION

For more than four hundred years it has stood as an awe-inspiring symbol of a prosperous, defiant city. People have come from the world over to marvel at its perfection, discuss its subtleties, and succumb to its magnetism.

Michelangelo created his masterpiece, the seventeen-foot-tall (over five meters) marble statue of David, between 1501 and 1504 for Florence, Italy—the city that was to become known as the cradle of the Renaissance. But unlike those who previously depicted the biblical hero, Michelangelo was not interested in portraying him in victory, having already slain his giant foe, Goliath.

Michelangelo chose as his subject David before the fight. This was a far more intriguing and rich subject. What would a young man, faced with imminent and overwhelming danger, look like?

What would be his body posture, his facial expression, his innermost thoughts in a moment of critical decision? Would he be paralyzed by fear or spurred on by a deep sense of purpose?

Michelangelo provides us with a fascinating answer. His young David stands tall in calm defiance. His countenance is that of determination, focus, scanning the scene before him for the most fitting strategy. He has made up his mind and is not backing down. And he seems to have full confidence in his own abilities to circumvent the looming, perilous situation that would fill other men with hopeless dread. He already knows that he will not fight his deadly foe head on, brute strength to brute strength. There would be no sense in that. Rather, he will redefine the rules of engagement in his own favor.

And so Michelangelo's *David* has come to represent not just the rebellious spirit of Florence but something far more encompassing: the notion of defying conventional wisdom, the thrill and power of overstepping traditional boundaries, and sweeping aside apparently immovable obstacles. In short, limitless possibilities. Over his left shoulder, David holds his weapon of choice for facing the hulking, heavily armed and battle-hardened adversary: a sling. It is his seemingly childish yet decisively effective resource for shedding conventionality.

The *American Heritage Dictionary of the English Language* defines a sling as:

(1) "a weapon consisting of a looped strap in which a stone is whirled and then let fly"

(2) "a slingshot."

Beyond the symbolic association with this epic hero, there are other compelling reasons why *Slingshot* was chosen as the title of this book. My purpose in writing it was to show a practical path to unconventional thinking and to inspire a reconnection with our natural, childhood creativity as the foundation for formulating successful strategies in adulthood.

The premise of the book is that continuous innovation is both necessary and exhilarating, and we all possess the inner capacity for it. Our capacity has simply been buried and lays dormant within us. As children, our imagination knew no boundaries. We would grab a slingshot and be instantly transformed into a warrior, a spy, a huntress or a protector of treasure. But as we grew older, our imagination was gradually reigned in, and our thinking eventually settled within the accepted boundaries of conventionality. It seems that our intellectual comfort zone has shifted from that of continuous exploration and inquisitiveness to that of conformity with accepted norms of adult perception.

A slingshot therefore is a fitting image of our childhood playfulness and lost, yet recoverable, creativity. By its very mechanics, it represents the alluring power of unconventional thinking. A slingshot works by applying tension to a pliable strip of material that launches a projectile forward. Similarly, unconventional thinking works by applying tension against taken-for-granted assumptions and perceived boundaries, and when unleashed, it propels us toward undiscovered market space and meaningful, new strategies.

**But a grown-up would always answer,
"That's a hat." Then I wouldn't talk about boa
constrictors or jungles or stars. I would put
myself on his level and talk about bridge and
golf and politics and neckties.**

In *The Little Prince*, French writer and aviator Antoine de Saint-Exupéry created one of those rare stories and literary characters that hold a timeless appeal and deep meaning for children and adults alike. The story is told through a narrator and depicts his encounter in the Sahara Desert with a diminutive visitor from another planet. In the beginning of the story the narrator recounts his first drawing at the age of six—that of an elephant having been swallowed whole by a boa constrictor. The drawing showed just the contours of an overstretched snake with the elephant inside, and therefore grown-ups were never frightened by the picture, which they mistook for that of a hat.

He then created a second drawing, this time of a transparent snake to make his meaning clear for adults.

Every time after that, whenever he encountered new grown-ups, he would test them by showing the first drawing. The grown-ups would invariably think it was a picture of a hat. Thus the narrator sadly realized that he could only talk with grown-ups about boring, pragmatic, superficial topics like politics and neckties rather than things that fueled his imagination. But when he unexpectedly meets the Little Prince in the middle of the desert and presents his first drawing, the extraterrestrial visitor immediately recognizes it as an elephant that's been swallowed by a boa constrictor.

Saint-Exupéry is clearly talking about the same void, the same disconnect between the creativity of childhood and the rigidity of adult thinking that I am targeting. But unlike in his story, my contention is that you don't have to be from another planet to bridge this void. You just need the right stimulus and framework—namely, the Slingshot Framework.

This book is laid out in the following sequence:

1. We Can't Get No Satisfaction

A perfectly and continuously satisfied consumer does not exist. At most, we can have an infatuated consumer. This realization is a powerful justification for you to never stop innovating. What is your absolute favorite product or service today? Now think about all the things that could make it even better.

2. Lifestyle Enrichment à la Carte

In order to keep consumers infatuated, you need to remain continuously relevant to them. How can you provide ongoing lifestyle enrichment?

3. Defying Conventional Wisdom

Many of the most powerful advances in human history have been done via acts of unconventional thinking. How can you recapture your childhood ingenuity to fuel unconventional thinking and become market driving?

4. Accordion Charts

How would you define your business from its most specific to most general utility? What are the various market spaces and competitors in between the two extremes? How can you collapse their best attributes into a new offering of exceptional value? How can you achieve relevance to the broadest spectrum of consumers? Let's do some visual accordion playing to find out.

5. Creating Blue Oceans

With insights gained through unconventional thinking, you are ready to create your Blue Oceans. Blue Ocean Strategy is a systematic approach for turning unconventional ideas into successful strategies. Why and how?

6. Proof of the Pudding

This final chapter packs real-life examples that demonstrate the string of concepts in action. Included are the fantastical creations of Dr. Seuss, Cow Parade's reinvention of public art, the super supercars of Christian Koenigsegg, followed by Tata's Nano, the world's most affordable vehicle. Also showcased are personal applications of the concepts, both in working with clients (Landslide and AkzoNobel) and in self-conceived initiatives (Team-O, a pioneering entertainment and media project, and the Immersive Executive Experience, a platform for multifaceted executive learning).

Appendix A: Radical Ideas

Suggestions on important social issues that could use some unconventional thinking.

Appendix B: Playful Habits for Grown-Ups

How-to tips for recovering your childhood creativity.

A dragon lives forever but not so little boys
Painted wings and giants' rings make way for other toys.
—"Puff the Magic Dragon," Lyrics by Leonard Lipton,
popularized by Peter, Paul, and Mary

The Slingshot Framework

Consumers by nature are insatiable; therefore, you need to keep them continuously or extendedly infatuated.

In order to infatuate, your offering must reflect compelling life-style or workstyle enrichment and stay relevant to consumers.

Ongoing lifestyle enrichment is achieved by daring to be market driving and to defy conventional wisdom. Reconnecting with your childhood creativity and sense of limitless exploration is your personal reservoir for this thinking process.

The Accordion Chart is a visual tool that enables you to channel unconventional thinking into strategic insights.

Such insights can be systematically shaped into successful strategies through the application of Blue Ocean Strategy.

The Slingshot Framework

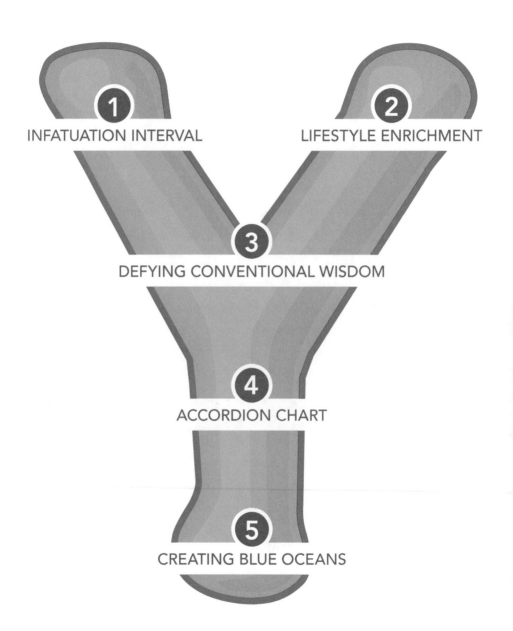

WE CAN'T GET NO SATISFACTION 1

We are always striving for things forbidden,
and covet those denied us.
—Ovid, Roman poet (43 BC–17 AD)

I would like to invite you to time travel with me. More precisely, I would like you to suppose that there is such a thing as time travel and, all of a sudden, a visitor from two hundred years ago appears in front of you. This visitor is naturally very curious about our world today and says, "Tell me about your world. What are some of the wonderful things that you have that I could not even imagine in my time?"

How would you respond?

After giving this question a bit of thought, you might say that today we can fly to any part of the world in less than a day. We can have our organs and joints replaced once they no longer function properly. We can buy anything anyone has to sell by a mere click of a button. We can order and pick up a sandwich or a cup of coffee through a window, made exactly as we like it.

Your visitor shakes his head in amazement and says: "Wow! I cannot believe that you have all that! You must be so content and satisfied to have such incredible things. Tell me, do you feel completely content and satisfied?"

Think about his question for a moment. Most likely, you would answer no, you don't feel particularly content or satisfied. In fact, you find air travel incredibly uncomfortable and inconvenient, recovery from medical procedures too long, the Internet unreliable and the drive-thru service of fast-food restaurants painfully slow.

Must Sell: Strange t-shirt with time travel powers

Now let's flip the scenario. Suppose that you were able to time travel two hundred years into the future. You would pose the same question to your host: "What are some of the most amazing things you have today that did not exist two hundred years ago?" Your host might respond by saying that he takes a pill once a week that detects and destroys most diseases before they even materialize in his body, stretching his life expectancy to four hundred years. Or he might say that with a snap of his fingers he can be instantly transported to Mars, and with another snap of his fingers he can be on Venus. Astounded and envious, you would go on to inquire, "Tell me, are you perfectly happy and fully satisfied?" Your host might answer, "Come to think of it, no! I really wish the little pill came in lime or lemon flavor instead of this intolerable raspberry. And on numerous occasions I've had to snap my fingers several times before I was finally lifted to Mars and Venus. It was very, very frustrating."

These two scenarios illustrate a fundamental facet of human nature: our marvelous insatiability, our continuous yearning for things that we don't yet possess. **As consumers, our satisfaction frontier is always just beyond our grasp.**

Note: For the sake of consistency, whenever possible I will use the term "consumer" to collectively mean target audience, customer, client, buyer, or purchaser.

Not surprisingly, children exhibit this trait in its most raw and pure form. I have just the three-year-old to prove it. My son Max loves trains with an absolute passion, especially Thomas the Tank Engine and his friends. Max has already accumulated a very impressive collection of the Thomas toy trains, one that handsomely eclipses the selection of most toy stores. But here is the fascinating thing. Every time Max receives a new train that he has obsessed about, which he had to have, he takes out the catalog that comes with the new train and promptly identifies the

next train that he absolutely can't live without. Once he acquired Fearless Freddie, Diesel 10 had to be next. And with Diesel 10 secured, Rocky surely could not be left wanting, and so on.

As parents, it's natural to anticipate after each purchase that Max will finally consider his collection complete and perfect as is. But for Max, what is equally natural is to expect his train portfolio to continue to expand indefinitely, or at least as long as he maintains his passion for them. And a big part of the thrill of building his collection in the first place is the possibility of its perpetual expansion and enhancement.

So here is the key point: **There is no such thing as a perfectly and continuously satisfied consumer.** Go ahead, test this on yourself. Think of your absolute favorite product that you have purchased or your very favorite service that you have experienced. Now ask yourself: Is your favorite product or favorite service experience absolutely perfect just the way it is, or could it somehow be better? Could you not think of any new attributes that would make your favorite things even more perfect for you? Of course you can. There are boundless possibilities for further

improvement, that create new layers of comfort, personalization, convenience, style, fun, harmony, security, simplicity, variety, and so forth to what you already have.

You may pose a possible objection here. There is in fact something that you consider perfect just the way it is. But what you are actually feeling is infatuation, not satisfaction. I will explain below.

First, let me share with you a couple of my favorite things: I am passionate about iTunes and have a close bond with my Samsonite Black Label carry-on travel bag. I love the idea that I can create a musical library of every piece of music that I like, no matter how eclectic, that I can easily browse and discover new music, and that each new song is so affordable. But I can also tell you half a dozen things that genuinely irritate me about iTunes, that I wish were different, such as the time limit for sampling songs prior to purchase, the inability to search for songs without knowing their exact titles, the continuous version upgrades, or all the music that is not yet accessible via iTunes.

Same with my Samsonite bag. I fly a lot, so my travel accessories are important to me. My Samsonite bag is great because it is super lightweight and durable, packs surprisingly well, and best of all, has a slick, distinctive, jet-black design. But what I find continuously bothersome is that the bag has no side pockets of any sort. I guess that would have compromised the ultracool design. As a result, I have to set down and unzip the entire bag every time I want to retrieve any of my travel essentials, such as my passport or the book I happen to be reading or my iPod. Why should I have to sacrifice or overlook basic convenience in exchange for all the things that I really like about the bag?

And here is the second key point: **While there is no such thing as a perfectly and continuously satisfied consumer, there is such a thing as an infatuated consumer.** As with personal relationships, infatuation occurs when consumers first come into contact with a product or a service that deeply resonates with them. Consequently, they become temporarily blinded by any shortcomings or possible defects and are in a trance of positive affiliation. Think of the first time you came into contact with a product or service that became one of your all-time favorite purchases. Remember how elated you felt and how that sense of complete elation gradually wore off with time?

Let me give you an illustration. A few years ago, airlines introduced individualized in-seat entertainment systems in economy-class cabins on intercontinental flights. Each passenger was presented with his own television screen in the seatback in front of him, along with a hand-held remote that allowed him to choose from dozens of movies, television shows, games, or musical selections. This was huge. It gave passengers control of how they would spend their time in the air. It instantaneously lifted the tedium of extended flying. Not surprisingly, the entertainment system caused a wave of excitement among passengers, who fully embraced its capabilities. But this elation did not last indefinitely. After a while, critical chatter then outright complaints started to creep into the cabin about the system, and then these complaints became more and more frequent. Why can't the system be activated more quickly? Why can't the movie and musical selections be changed more frequently? Why aren't the screens brighter and easier to see?

Think about the progression here. In the beginning, passengers welcomed the innovation of an individualized entertainment system with childlike gratitude and giddiness. But as its novelty began to wear off, they started to notice and voice its apparent shortcomings and how it could be made even better. They were no longer satisfied just with having their own systems; they demanded it be perfected further.

What happens when consumers start to express dissatisfaction and their comments go unanswered? There are a couple of possibilities. One, if they have the opportunity, consumers will eventually turn away from the offering altogether. For example, in the case of the in-flight entertainment system, more and more passengers are bringing their own mobile music, game, and movie players onboard, thereby opting out of using the built-in systems altogether. But even if consumers don't fully turn away or are not yet in a position to do so, they become more and more reluctant users—so they voice their displeasure more and more and their affinity for the offering less and less, continuously turning from fans into disgruntled critics. Which is what may happen with me unless iTunes finds a way to address what I perceive to be its weaknesses, or if a new carry-on bag catches my eye that is just as cool as my Samsonite but much more user friendly.

The other possibility, which is much more rare, intriguing, and unpredictable, is that consumers will take matters into their own hands and change the utility of an offering for themselves. Consider the following extreme example.

In 1994, seventy-three-year-old Alvin Straight drove his '66 John Deere lawnmower 250 miles (400 km) from Lauren, Iowa, to Mount Zion, Wisconsin, to see his ailing brother. He made this choice because his eyesight was too poor to qualify for a driver's license, and he was too proud to hitchhike. Going along at five miles per hour (8 km/h), he met numerous interesting people along the way. His journey was a national sensation and the subject of a major 1999 movie by David Lynch, entitled *Straight Story*.

To be sure, through his radical act, Alvin Straight was not express-ing his satisfaction with John Deere mowers per se, but rather his frustration with the general lack of transportation options for his particular predicament. In desperation, he created an entire new utility for the mower.

Such unexpected bursts of consumer ingenuity may unveil completely new strategic horizons for companies. Should John Deere consider getting into the business of personal transport? Does Alvin represent a previously overlooked, sizable consumer group? Is a transition to this kind of business application possible or feasible? Asking such questions is what stimulates explora-tion beyond existing market boundaries, allowing companies to drive markets and achieve continuous relevance. But I am getting ahead of myself.

Even more extreme is the story of Larry Walters, a California truck driver. One day in 1982, Larry had a free afternoon, and he decided to create some excitement for himself. He rigged forty-five weather balloons to his lawn chair, packed a lunch, grabbed a BB gun, planted himself in the chair, and ceremoniously released the supporting ropes. He estimated that he would rise about thirty feet (10 meters) and gently levitate over his garden for a couple of hours. Instead, he quickly ascended to the incredible height of sixteen thousand feet (approximately 5,000 meters). After a while he got cold and scared, shot some of the balloons in order to descend, drifted over the Los Angeles airport (interfering with air traffic), and crashed into power lines as he came down (knocking out power to some parts of the city). In this case, I think Larry acted not out of desperation but perhaps boredom or curiosity. He clearly was not satisfied with the more banal and conventional use of a lawn chair, and he took it upon himself to transform it into a cockpit.

What I am describing here is a clear transition by consumers in their relationships with offerings that surround them. Any well-received offering first finds itself in an **Infatuation Interval** at which consumers just can't get enough of it. However, this interval is by nature fleeting, and with few exceptions, it gives way to the **Entitlement Period**, in which consumers feel entitled to all of the offering's perceived benefits and demand more.

Nintendo's Wii is a great example of an offering that has created an extended Infatuation Interval. Consumers were so infatuated with the Wii that during the bleak holiday season of 2008, a full two years after its market introduction, it still doubled its sales volume from that of a year before. There was so much extra demand that the secondary market price for the $250 unit was at a $100 premium on the Internet. Clearly, consumers just could not get enough.

Here is some humorous proof of the Wii's lingering infatuation hold. There was a news blip on Tampa Bay Online in September 2009 about a mishandled police raid earlier in the year of a con-

victed drug dealer's home near Lakeland, Florida. Apparently, within twenty minutes of entering the empty house, some investigators noticed a Wii video bowling game lying around and found it too irresistible to ignore. They began bowling frame after frame. As

Caught on Tape: Infatuated officers

the article points out: "A Polk County sheriff's detective cataloging evidence repeatedly put down her work and picked up a Wii remote to bowl. When she hit two strikes in a row, she raised her arms above her head, jumping and kicking. The detectives did not know that a wireless security camera connected to a computer inside the home was recording their activity."

Even though it looks bad, you can't blame the officers. After all, they were still trapped within the Infatuation Interval of the Wii and obviously under its spell. So they were hardly responsible for their irresponsible conduct.

Or consider the Infatuation Interval created by the novel *The Da Vinci Code*, which remained a worldwide cultural sensation for years following its 2003 debut. Despite lacking a fully original central theme in the book (it is comparable to that of *Holy Blood Holy Grail* by Michael Baigent from twenty-one years prior), Dan Brown's unique combination of suspense, history, art, mysticism, religion, romance, and adventure travel absolutely captivated audiences worldwide. The book is the best-selling English language novel of the twenty-first century, and Dan Brown was recognized as one of the one hundred most influential people of 2005 by *Time* magazine.

It is interesting to note that the Infatuation Interval and Entitlement Period for children seem to overlap instead of being sequential, perhaps because their concept of time hasn't fully developed yet. Think back to my son Max, who is simultaneously infatuated by a new train he receives and is already marking in the catalog the next train he must possess, without which his collection seems imperfect.

Dr. Seuss (a.k.a. Theodor Geisel), the American writer and illustrator of children's books whom I reference numerous times in this book, holds a similar distinction to that of Saint-Exupéry. His books are evergreen favorites of children and adults alike, and his invented characters have deep meaning about human nature. In his story about Sneetches, he introduces two types of these fantastical creatures. Ones with red stars on their bellies and ones without. What those without stars desire the most in the world is to have stars themselves, which of course is impossible. At least until an enterprising, high-energy character by the name of Sylvester McMonkey McBean rolls into town with a strange contraption that can magically stamp stars. But alas, as soon as all the bare Sneetches get stars on their stomachs, those who originally had stars on their bellies no longer want theirs. So their stars are magically removed by McBean's machine, at which point the other group wants their stars removed. And so this cycle continues over and over, until all the Sneetches run out of money and finally realize that it doesn't really matter if they have stars or not. While this story has numerous connotations, its relevance here is this: McBean was able to instantaneously provide the Sneetches with exactly the offering they obsessed about, that infatuated them the most at any particular moment. And for their part, the Sneetches could never remain satisfied once they received their foremost wish; they always wanted what they didn't have. Sound familiar?

How can you tell if the Infatuation Interval of your offering is starting to fade? Keep a close eye on your consumers and monitor how their perception of your offering is evolving. For example, here is a telling sign that the current Infatuation Interval for BlackBerry devices is nearing its end: a survey conducted by online market researchers Crowd Science in March 2010 revealed that 39 percent of BlackBerry owners would definitely or probably switch to an iPhone once their subscriptions expired. Why? Because BlackBerry devices have acquired a perception of being too serious and too business oriented and lacking a fun factor—which is the very dimension driving the current surge of consumer infatuation with smartphones.

Notice I said above that Infatuation Intervals turn into Entitlement Periods—with a few exceptions. What are these exceptions? There are certain offerings that may hold an almost permanent infatuation for consumers. Many of these derive from a strong childhood association that may stay with consumers for life. For example, always eating Heinz ketchup with your favorite meals as a child could spark a lifelong attachment to it, which would explain why someone as an adult would be reluctant to travel to any country where it is not available. That is a pretty strong and potentially permanent infatuation.

A lasting infatuation could form during adulthood as well. A certain offering grabs you just the right way at the right time to keep you continuously infatuated. The interesting thing with such lasting infatuations is that consumers actually become very territorial about the offering, but with the opposite connotations of fleeting infatuations. With the latter, infatuation transitions to entitlement, when the consumers start to demand improvement. With the former, consumers feel entitled to the permanence of their infatuation, and hence they demand that the offering stay unchanged. So any company must understand the risk of upsetting its permanently infatuated consumers when looking to alter its offering. Just ask Coke about this, when it tried to tinker with its one-hundred-year-old formula in 1985, causing a backlash from outraged consumers and forcing the company to leave it just the way it was, under the evocative label Coca-Cola Classic.

You may also be wondering about the role that your offering's price plays in causing infatuation. It becomes a strategic component at your disposal. As part of the right combination of attributes, both pricing extremes can help to induce infatuation. A low strategic price point can be an infatuation enabler to a mass of new consumers who consider access to your offering as a life-enriching experience. This is the case with the Nano, the world's most affordable car, whose story I will discuss in the last chapter. A high strategic price point, on the other hand, can act as an aphrodisiac to those who can afford it. After all, a high price is linked to a perception of status and quality.

A good illustration of this perceived link between high price and infatuation can be found in a recent experiment by the California Institute of Technology. They orchestrated a wine tasting among inexperienced wine drinkers in which $90 bottles were labeled alternatively at their real price and at $10, while $5 wines were marked at their real price and at $45. During the tasting, the brain activity of participants was measured to see the level of pleasure they felt. According to Yahoo News, the results showed: "The part of the brain that reacts to a pleasant experience responded more strongly to pricey wines than cheap ones—even when tasters were given the same vintage in disguise. Apparently, raising the price really does make the wine taste better."

Your pricing options don't stop here. What about removing it altogether? In 2007 the Irish rock band Radiohead sold its newest album over the Internet without a fixed price, for whatever consumers were willing to pay. This gimmick had an infatuating effect not only because of its novelty but also because it was empowering for consumers: it put them in complete control of exactly how much they thought something was worth, how much they were willing to spend on it. The move was subsequently copied by restaurants, hotels, and cinemas with the effect of raising consumer traffic and publicity. Perhaps somewhat surprisingly, the average price consumers ended up paying of their own volition turned out to be just slightly less than the provider's target price for the offerings.

What are the overall takeaways in terms of strategy and business application?

1 Any highly successful and well-received offering that you put on the market transitions from an Infatuation Interval to the Entitlement Period, barring those that create a permanent infatuation. During the Infatuation Interval, consumers are fixated on the offering's novelty, seduced by its perceived benefits, and blinded to its potential shortcomings.

2 As the veil of infatuation wears off, consumers gradually take ownership of the offering, that is to say, they will no longer consider themselves privileged but rather fully entitled to it. The perception of ownership passes from provider to consumer. Consumers feel that they now possess full rights of ownership for the offering. This is the start of the Entitlement Period, in which consumers will take notice of and express all the things that could make the offering even better for them. And you have to be careful here: if you let your consumers linger too long in the Entitlement Period without heeding their suggestions or demands, they will at some point turn away from your offering altogether. That is the danger of stopping to innovate, especially in today's environment of accelerated life cycles, market convergence, and relentless inundation of consumers by an overabundance of offerings—all of which puts immense pressure on your offering to retain the attention of consumers.

3 One strategic target, therefore, is to extend the Infatuation Interval of your offering as much as possible. For example, think about the extended Infatuation Interval of Nintendo's Wii, which captured the imagination and the passion of an entirely new, massive consumer segment—that of previous nongamers. Ponder the same for *The Da Vinci Code*, which was a worldwide sensation for years after its publication. Be mindful to recognize if your offering goes as far as producing a significant number of permanently infatuated consumers who feel entitled to having your offering remain unchanged.

4 A second strategic target is to have an ongoing process of innovation so that you create a continuous stream of Infatuation Intervals for consumers. In other words, as soon as the Infatuation Interval for your current offering is nearing its end, you tweak its features and utility in a way that a new

Infatuation Interval is created. You can do this based on consumer feedback from early adopters who have already transitioned to the Entitlement Period. Or, more powerfully, you
can think about and anticipate latent consumer desires, which
consumers themselves are unable to express. In this case you
enter the realm of market driving rather than market driven,
which allows you to occupy undiscovered market space. In
the famous words of Henry Ford: "If I'd asked the consumer
what they wanted, they'd have said a faster horse." Unless, of
course, he happened to ask a Larry Walters or an Alvin Straight.

5 A third strategic target is to create infectious infatuations so
that you are not just recaptivating your existing consumers but
increasingly attracting previous nonconsumers as well.

Here is a challenge for you. Let's consider again our time traveler from two hundred years ago and his question about some of the most wonderful things we have today. Now think about what it would take for someone answering this question to cite your company's offering in their response. Moreover, when asked the follow-up question about their level of satisfaction and contentment, what would it take for them to respond that they feel completely infatuated with your offering?

There is no such thing as a perfectly and continuously satisfied consumer, but there can be such a thing as a perpetually infatuated consumer. It is up to you to find a way to keep them infatuated. In the chapter that follows, I will talk about how to formulate your offering so that it has the best likelihood of infatuating.

As a quick reminder and reference, the Slingshot Framework chart at the end of each chapter highlights the topic just covered:

The Slingshot Framework

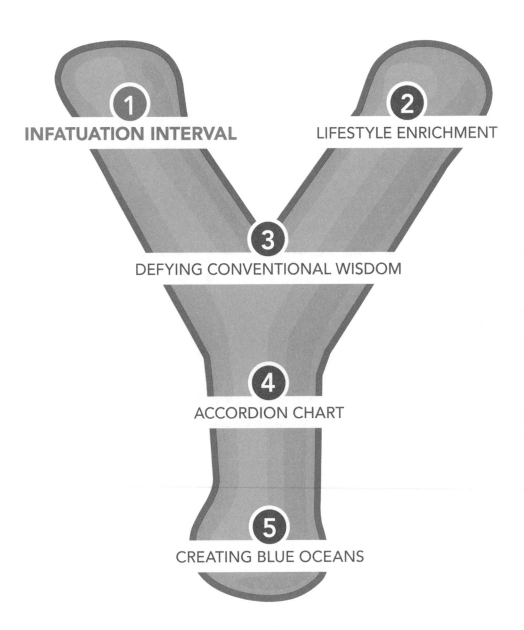

Have you visited **www.slingshotliving.com** lately?
If not, you're missing half the fun and learning.

LIFESTYLE ENRICHMENT À LA CARTE 2

If you don't like change, you're going
to like irrelevance even less.
—General Eric Shinseki,
former U.S. Army Chief of Staff

So how do you mold infatuated consumers? What do you need to provide in order to capture their attention, their imagination, and their affection at the same time?

As a way of exploring the answers to these questions, consider your current offering. If your consumers were asked to name their ten favorite purchases across all products and services, in your estimation how many of them would include your offering on their list? If you don't think that your consumers cherish you enough to be in their top ten, how can you expect to infatuate them? After all, consumers have a capacity to bond closely or identify themselves tightly with just a handful of offerings. So if you want to infatuate them, your competition is all the other offerings that are blocking you from being in their top ten. And if you are in their top ten, why not aim to be number one—the offering that your consumers consider their most favorite, the most indispensable? Because once you are at the top of the list, your strategic possibilities open up immensely. You now possess the full attention and hearts of your consumers, and they will follow you across market spaces and industries. The connection becomes so strong that they will link themselves not just to your offering but to your brand behind the offering, and therefore, they will be receptive to consuming anything you offer that is consistent with their brand expectations. Moreover, they will be your brand ambassadors toward nonconsumers.

Here's a case in point. Think back to iTunes, which I mentioned was one of my favorite things in chapter 1. The concept of iTunes was so compelling that since its 2001 introduction it has inspired a continuous extension of related offerings, including various new versions of the iPod itself, all kinds of accessories, the iPhone, and most recently the iPad. Consumers track Apple across this family of interrelated offerings because they all reinforce and expand their close connection with the "i" brand that iTunes popularized. They are staying infatuated. As proof, observe the near cultish hype and media frenzy surrounding Steve Jobs's periodic unveiling of the company's latest creation, the next member of the iFamily to hit the market.

Another example is the Virgin Group. Founded in 1970 by Richard Branson as a music mail-order business, the first Virgin Records shop was opened a year later. Today, Virgin is one of the most recognized global brands, and the group is involved in diverse businesses ranging from music to mobile telephony, transportation, travel, financial services, media, and fitness. They succeeded in branding their lifestyle concept of sophisticated fun, which they replicated consistently across market spaces in a way that consumers followed. Virgin's next lifestyle-driving frontier is to make space travel accessible to the public. Virgin Galactic calls itself the first spaceline and aspires to give consumers the cathartic experience of looking back on earth from above, continuing to stretch the mortal limits of its infatuating brand.

Now ask yourself this: besides a business-sparking infatuation, can an infatuation give birth to a substantial business? You bet! Twenty years ago European football was largely a seasonal sport. There were fall and spring seasons with well-defined breaks in the summer and winter months. Today, it is played virtually year round, and the sport enjoys immense popularity worldwide. A key driver of this development was the English club Manchester United, which rightfully calls itself "the world's most popular football team." What MU realized was that they were sitting on a gold mine. They had a captive audience that was fanatical about their football club. They needed to turn the fan base of a seasonal pastime into a year-round entertainment and lifestyle platform. And that is exactly what they did. In its annual list of the world's most valuable sports teams, Forbes ranked MU not only as the richest football club in the world but the most valuable team in any sport—pegged at a cool $1.8 billion market value, with yearly revenues of $500 million. In 2010 the club earned the top spot for the second year running, followed by the likes of the Dallas Cowboys and New York Yankees, both valued at $1.6 billion. According to David Gill, MU's chief executive, MU boasts more than 300 million fans worldwide, of which more than 130 million are active members: 80 million in Asia and 10 million in North America, indicating that they have created a truly worldwide appeal. And the club's television channel is shown in over 190 million homes.

These are simply amazing figures! How many companies can you think of with this sort of fan base? It is an immense global community whose members' self-perception and world outlook revolves in large part around their devotion to MU.

Take a look at www.manutd.com, the club's website. If you think you are visiting the homepage of a mere football club, you are in for a shock. A maze of offerings tied to the club's octopus-like brand awaits you: MU Mobile Communications, MU Television, MU Travel, Conferences and Event Hosting Services at MU Stadium, the MU Foundation, MU Megastore, and MU Finance (meaning you can actually take out MU-branded car and home insurance, mortgages, and credit cards). In essence, this community is being blanketed by a complete bubble of MU-related offerings, all of which reinforce their infatuation with the football team.

Consider these two questions:

1 If you can captivate consumers as MU has done, is there any limit to what you can sell them? Would not this same community be interested in traveling on MU Airlines or welcoming a new line of MU health drinks? Not only is this question useful for you to identify continuous brand expansion opportunities, but it also helps you to identify your most relevant competitors of tomorrow. Would an insurance provider or a mortgage company have thought of MU as a viable competitor a decade ago? Your competitors of tomorrow can come from anywhere, so you better look all around.

2 If this vast group of 130 million consumers identify themselves as active members of the MU community, how many additional brands do they have the capacity to feel a strong affinity for at the same time? In other words, you need to understand the infatuation draw of your offering in relation to those of other offerings as well as the saturation level of target consumers. Because in this case, you are up against the MU juggernaut for the hearts and attention of these 130 million consumers around the world.

Of course, one of the most enduring infatuations surrounding a company is Harley-Davidson. Its fan club, calling themselves the Harley Owners Group (or HOG for short) has one million members worldwide. In 2003, a quarter of a million people came to Harley-Davidson's centennial anniversary celebration at its home base in

Milwaukee, Wisconsin. They all wanted to be part of this historic milestone. Notice here again that, above all, Harley-Davidson aficionados identify themselves in terms of their association with their motorcycle and related accessories. Their world revolves around Harley to such an extent that they actively cultivate an entire HOG way of being.

And Harley-Davidson feels and stokes this love. In 1987, it made business history by petitioning the International Trade Commission for early termination of the five-year tariff on foreign-made heavyweight motorcycles, which artificially protected its monopoly in the United States. In essence, Harley-Davidson was so confident of its distinctive market position that it did not view foreign manufacturers as real competition, and it wanted the floodgates opened to prove it. Through 2006 the company posted twenty-one consecutive years of revenue growth, indicative of its extended courtship with consumers. Yet even a company with such an enviable lifestyle aura and fan base must continuously strive to stay relevant. Harley-Davidson hit a bump in 2007 and 2008 and must now figure out ways to attract younger generations without upsetting its more mature core followers.

What then is the strategic commonality among these examples of mass infatuations and resulting brand extensions? What do all these companies share?

I can answer this question in two words: **lifestyle enrichment**. These companies all understand that they are not in the business of making a certain product or providing a certain service, but rather they offer something much more encompassing, much more fundamental: they are in the business of enriching people's lives. They are in the business of making people's lives more fun, more thrilling, simpler, more comfortable, more liberating, safer, more meaningful, more efficient, and more harmonious. This seemingly small shift in strategic thinking is huge. It allows companies to infatuate large groups of consumers and to do so continuously.

Now recall an important point from the end of the previous chapter: do not be limited in looking to your current consumers as the source of new lifestyle-enriching ideas. When consulted, most consumers respond based on what they already have rather than expressing desires for things that don't yet exist. Instead, you need to observe how both consumers and nonconsumers live, work, and play, and anticipate their latent needs and desires. As Steve Jobs puts it: "It's hard for users to tell you what they want when they've never seen anything remotely like it." Or consider Denys Lasdun, a leading twentieth-century English architect, who observed that the architect's job is to give a client "not what he wants but what he never dreamed that he wanted; and when he gets it, he recognizes it as something he wanted all the time."

How about this for anticipating latent, life-enriching needs? In the 1990s, shortly after the fall of communism, scores of Ukrainians

packed into buses headed for central European destinations, such as Budapest, where they could buy all kinds of Western consumer products for the first time. Eventually, these elaborate shopping excursions caught the attention of the Ukrainian underground. Packs of bandits started raiding the buses in midjourney, knowing that they were full of cash on the way out or full of goods on the way back home.

As this ritual evolved, empathetic bandits began issuing certificates to their victims that documented they had been robbed. In this manner, if the bus was intercepted again, the passengers could legitimately prove to the next group of robbers that they had already been cleaned out and were not trying to hide anything. As such, the certificates saved time and confusion, and by overstepping the traditional boundaries of banditry, they provided a much safer, more efficient, and therefore more enriching overall experience for the victims.

Let's look at the concept of lifestyle enrichment with children. First, kids have a wonderfully fertile imagination that allows them to create their own enrichment. They can assign magical powers and fabricate elaborate stories around common household items or experiences—turn a broom into an enchanted sword in the blink of an eye or jump off a couch as though it were a hovering rescue helicopter. In this way, children can formulate and retain a deep affinity for even the most mundane objects or experiences. This is the type of connection that companies covet to establish between their offerings and consumers. If only we retained our childlike powers of imagination as adults, how much easier it would be for companies to make such connections.

In another sense, children give themselves over to immersive experiences to a much greater extent than adults do. As I mentioned previously, my son Max can't get enough of all things having to do with Thomas the Tank Engine. He feels more enriched by the entire experience of comprehensive and interrelated Thomas the Tank Engine stimuli: toy trains, tracks, puzzles, television shows, apparel, educational books, cards, stickers, accessories, and online videos. He indulges in them fully. By the way, Max recently got his very own e-mail account. Can you guess what he asked his e-mail address to start with? "Lovesthomas@"!

I would argue that a large component of the strong lifestyle enrichment created by the likes of Manchester United or Virgin or Harley-Davidson is that their offerings contain powerful elements that reconnect us with our childhood: playing, exploring, discovering, a sense of freedom, fun, and self-expression. **How can you create dimensions for your offering that speak to childhood desires and gratifying memories?**

It's more intuitive to see how the lifestyle enrichment perspective applies to business-to-consumer businesses (B2C), but how about heavy manufacturing or business-to-business (B2B) companies? In fact, the perspective has even more diverse applications for the latter. Why would that be the case?

First, tweaking the label slightly, any B2B company should consider the **workstyle enrichment** impact of its offerings on its direct customers. How does your offering help to make the work of your corporate customer more efficient, more meaningful, safer, simpler, more comfortable, more fun, more eco-friendly? A good illustration of the power of this perspective is Landslide

Technologies, whose story will be featured in detail in the final chapter. As a start-up in 2006, Landslide entered the already saturated market space of sales force automation (systems designed to track the sales activities of an organization) that was dominated by such titans as Microsoft, SAP, Oracle, Siebel, and Salesforce. com. Landslide, however, quickly became recognized as a trailblazer by providing workstyle enrichment features to clients. In fact, boldly overstepping traditional industry boundaries, the company labeled its offering *sales workstyle management* and was the first to offer such dimensions as a VIP service, a twenty-four-hour call center that allowed salesmen on the road to dictate the results of their field activities to a live person. This service empowered salesmen to multitask, thus adding layers of efficiency, comfort, and even fun to their workstyle.

Second, the offering of most any B2B company is a conduit to a final B2C offering. For example, at the end of a manufacturing chain there usually resides a targeted retail consumer. So, as a company at the beginning or in the middle of the chain, if you can consider and help drive the lifestyle enrichment impact of the final retail offering, then you can solidify the indispensability of the entire chain. Let's revisit the individualized in-flight entertainment system that I talked about in the previous chapter. In this example, the company supplying the system ought to focus heavily on the lifestyle enrichment impact of its offering on end users (airline passengers) as a way of creating an indispensible offering for direct customers (airplane manufacturers) and their subsequent customers (commercial airlines). I mentioned how the system was very well received in the beginning by passengers. However, their infatuation appeared to transition briskly to entitlement and expressions of dissatisfaction, perhaps bringing into question the long-term value of the investment made by airplane manufacturers and airlines in installing the system. What could have been done better?

Here is one possibility of how the manufacturer seemingly failed to fully consider the lifestyle enrichment impact on passengers as well as the workstyle implications on flight attendants. Each individualized entertainment system is operated by a handheld remote. In the middle of the remote, mixed in with all the buttons that provide system functionality, is the flight attendant call button. Think about it. What is that button doing there? How might consumers actually use it? In practice, airline passengers started pushing all the buttons in rapid succession. Invariably they pushed the attendant call button by accident, not knowing its purpose. When the button was pushed, a loud, shrill, ringing sound reverberated throughout the cabin. When three hundred passengers (including numerous children) were doing this, the sound is set off repeatedly for the duration of an intercontinental flight, disrupting both the enjoyment of those trying to use the entertainment system and those trying to sleep or relax.

Within a few months of the system's introduction, I asked flight attendants on several flights how they viewed the call button's functionality. One told me that due to its constant, accidental activation, she became completely immune to its sound and ignored it altogether. Another said that the airline had deactivated the entire call button function rather than endure its continuous, bothersome beeping.

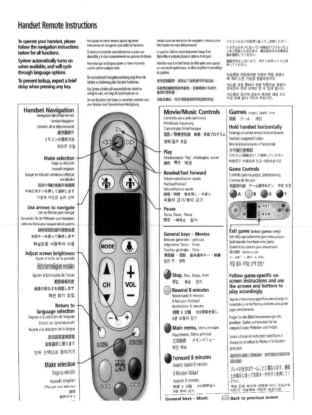

Look closely. Can you identify the rogue flight-attendant calling button?

In essence, this seemingly insignificant and unnecessary oversight created an immediate pushback, endangering the entertainment system's Infatuation Interval for every constituent group on the flight: passengers trying to enjoy its benefits, passengers not wanting to engage with it, and the airline crew running the flight. If only the manufacturer had considered the full lifestyle and workstyle implications of its offering, such negative reaction could have been easily avoided. For example, what if the flight attendant call button were placed somewhere else? Or what if the button needed to be pushed twice in order to activate the sound, making it less likely that someone would press it by accident? Or what if the call button triggered only a visual or localized signal?

Third, B2B companies can consider new B2C applications of their offerings, thus bypassing their current intermediaries altogether, to focus directly on creating lifestyle enrichment for an entirely new set of end consumers. Take the example of Kuka Industries, Europe's largest manufacturer of automated industrial machines. In 2000, some Kuka engineers looking at the company's KR500, a robot designed to lift car parts, let their imagination wonder and asked, "What if we could attach a chair to the end of it? It could make a fun ride." The result of their unleashed imagination was the Robocoaster, a joyride capable of 1.4 million programmable twists, which the company calls the world's first passenger-carrying robot. Since 2002, it's been installed at amusement parks around the world and appeared in blockbuster action films such as *Die Another Day, The Da Vinci Code, Thunderbirds,* and *Tomb Raider.* The foray into this new lifestyle enrichment application has given birth to the Kuka Entertainment business unit, helping to buoy the company's performance from the vicissitudes of the auto industry. So ponder this: How can you get your offering to be featured in the next James Bond film? Or a bit more broadly, how can your B2B business be a continuous source of both workstyle and lifestyle enrichment?

One of the best examples of a manufacturing company where the pursuit of lifestyle enrichment is part of the organization's soul is W. L. Gore. This privately owned company makes a wide range of products that serve numerous industries because it encourages employees to cross-pollinate ideas and come up with completely new applications for its technologies. Among its products are Gore-Tex (the breathable, water- and windproof synthetic fabric), Glide dental floss (the first floss to resist shredding), and Elixir guitar strings (which last three to five times longer than normal strings).

Fast Company magazine commented: "Gore's first marketing coup came with Gore-Tex. For Gore, which in essence is a component manufacturer, the challenge was to find a way to outflank the middlemen and talk directly to potential consumers—the people who buy clothing in retail stores. Gore simply sold the laminated fabrics to apparel manufacturers, which in turn relied on retailers. The solution: Gore created tags for the final garments that said

'Gore-Tex: Guaranteed to Keep You Dry.' This pathbreaking idea was later copied in the 1990s by Intel, with its 'Intel Inside' ad campaign and its conspicuous stickers on personal computers."

I can share with you a couple of my personal experiences where the provider was clearly missing a compelling lifestyle enriching justification for its offering.

My family spends summers at the idyllic beachside community of Higgins Beach, Maine. Due to its northerly location, the high season is quite short, lasting from 4th of July to Labor Day. A few summers ago, I went to pick up a couple of things at the only convenience shop in the community but was taken aback by the rather outrageous markups on each item. When I questioned the proprietor, rather than trying to justify his pricing policies based on the high value of convenience offered by his store's strategic location, he answered: "Well, now, I somehow have to make enough money during the short summer season to last me the whole year, don't I?"

Another example is when I called the customer support group of my phone company to seek help in understanding their over-complicated billing statement. The agent on the phone was very pleasant and was able to answer each of my questions. At the end of the call, I asked her, "You have been very helpful in explaining everything, but I am curious if it would be possible to make the statements simple enough so that customers wouldn't need to call for help in order to decipher them?" She responded, "Well, yes, I suppose we could do that, but then I would be out of a job!" I wondered afterward if a supervisor listening in on the call would praise or reprimand her for this very honest, though rather unfulfilling, answer.

In contrast, let's consider a dimension that has alluring lifestyle implications: simplicity. An interesting consequence of the often overwhelming choices, rapid change, and complexity that consumers see among offerings is the attractiveness of simplification. Think about the refreshingly basic design and ease of use of the Google homepage or the iPod or the Flip. The Flip is a camcorder that came on the scene in 2007 on the heels of increasingly complex and functionality-packed competitors. Its core strategic focus is to provide consumers with a streamlined and simplified way of creating personal videos, and everything about the product reinforces this theme. *BusinessWeek* observed: "Flip designers had a test—whenever they created a prototype and handed it to someone, they intended for that person to be able to turn it on and play with it in 30 seconds without having to read a manual. The 30-second rule became very important. Instead of adding lots of features, designers limited the Flip to four buttons: on/off, record, playback, and delete. That philosophy is still in place. To keep the user experience simple, everything needed to play the device is built in (including a pop-out USB arm to connect the device to a computer). It allows the camera to ship with no installation CD and no cables. Everything the user needs is contained in the camera."

Amazingly, the Flip has been the best-selling camcorder on Amazon.com since the day of its debut, capturing about 13 percent of the camcorder market, and it accounted for 36 percent of all camcorders sold during the 2009 holiday season, according to market researcher NPD Group. The power of simplicity, indeed.

Dying Newspaper Trend Buys Nation's Newspapers Three More Weeks

WASHINGTON—A recent glut of feature stories on the death of the American newspaper has temporarily made the outmoded form of media appealing enough to stave off its inevitable demise for an additional 21 days, sources reported Monday. "People really seem to identify with these moving, 'end-of-an-era'-type pieces," *Washington Post* editor-in-chief Leonard Downie, Jr. said. "It's nice to see that the printed word is still, at least for now, the most powerful medium for reporting on the death of the printed word." Downie added that the poignant farewell Op-Ed he recently penned was so well received that he will be able to hold onto his job for up to six more days.

This satirical short from the Onion pokes fun at the looming obsolescence of newspapers. To be sure, they are in a tight spot. There are now more enriching news sources for the younger generation, such as *The Daily Show* with Jon Stewart on Comedy Central, and more convenient and real-time platforms for accessing news, such as the Internet and handheld devices.

As this example illustrates, in order for companies to deliver lifestyle enrichment to consumers, being relevant is much more important than being best in any traditional measure. You can publish the best newspaper on the market, but it won't matter if newspapers themselves are becoming irrelevant and no longer enriching people's evolving lifestyles. At most, you can prolong your inevitable demise and have the dubious honor of being the last newspaper to fold.

Another example of the distinction between being relevant and being best is that of Coke and Pepsi. Coke has perpetually ruled the carbonated soft drink market space, with Pepsi being number two. Rather than continuing to fight an uphill battle for supremacy within this space, Pepsi instead decided to branch out strategically. It began focusing more on consumer relevance, diversifying into beverages more connected to healthy living. In the process it acquired such brands as Gatorade and Tropicana. By the end of 2005, Pepsi derived only 20 percent of its total revenues from carbonated drinks, compared to Coke's 80 percent, and its market valuation overtook Coke's for the first time—even though just ten years before Coke's value was three times that of Pepsi. In essence Pepsi conceded the narrower confines of the carbonated beverage market to Coke, and by doing so it became the more broadly relevant and therefore arguably the more successful company.

Certainly if being relevant is more important than being best, then it is also more important than being biggest. You have to look no further than General Motors. After succumbing to a perfect storm of market conditions, GM filed for bankruptcy in June 2009, making it the biggest industrial failure in U.S. history, needing $50 billion in government assistance as a lifeline. In the same month, it was removed (along with Citibank) from the Dow Jones Industrial 30 Index (a basket of the most prestigious, publicly traded U.S. companies). Yet just two years back, in 2007, GM was the largest car company in the world *and* the biggest U.S. manufacturing entity with over $200 billion in revenues. The bigger they are, the harder and quicker they can fall—if the flame of continuous lifestyle relevance is extinguished.

A few years ago at the Fortune Innovation Forum in New York City, I heard Chris Bangle, then chief designer for BMW, make an observation that really struck me. He said that in today's economy every consumer is a de facto designer. When consumers make a purchase, be it a car, a handheld device, or an African safari vacation, they have the option and the responsibility to customize it to their individual tastes. In other words, consumers are being increasingly empowered to get things just as they want them. And along with this power comes the new responsibility of being part of the design process, rather than just purchasing off-the-shelf, prefab offerings. Think about your most recent mobile phone purchase and the myriad of options from which to select your ringtone or wallpaper image. And if that wasn't enough, you can also upload your own ringtone or wallpaper, making the choices literally endless. **Therefore, the goal of companies focused on sustained relevance is no longer to make the perfect design but to create a platform that allows consumers to make the perfect design for themselves in a meaningful yet simple manner.**

I will elaborate on the strategic issue of sustained relevance in a later chapter on Accordion Charts, which is a visual tool to help companies continuously examine and broaden the indispensability of their offerings in the marketplace.

As thought-provoking as Chris's insight is of itself, there is a deeper meaning and connection related to my premise about our dormant childhood creativity. Think about it. Up until now, what I have been saying is that we all have boundless ingenuity as children, which we gradually disconnect from as we grow up. We live and think within narrow boundaries as adults, in the false conviction that we no longer have any use for our childlike perspectives. But if what Chris is saying is right, then this entire linear equation is being fundamentally challenged by the evolution of our society. We are moving away from cookie-cutter offerings to ones that not only enable but in fact require adults to create their own designs and fabricate their own customizations. Which is what we did as children. So, in fact, we are in the midst of coming full circle, which has profound implications. We not only need an injection of our former resourcefulness to create continuously relevant offerings, but we also need it to be able to receive them as well. Therefore, reengaging our childhood creativity is not just an imperative part of successful business strategy. It is now also an imperative part of a full consumer experience.

To illustrate this shift, consider these examples of what front-running companies are doing to fully empower consumers to customize. *BusinessWeek* observed in April 2010:

> *Kids with LEGO sets were once content to follow instructions and assemble a toy. If the picture on the box was a battleship, that's what you built— unless you decided to skip the instructions, mix in other blocks, and build mutant battleships instead. LEGO's DesignByME site brings some order to this chaos, offering digital design tools so kids can create a toy entirely from their imagination. When satisfied, they simply zip their creation to the company.*

LEGO will then manufacture the parts and send them in a box the kids also designed.

As far back as 1999, Nike began letting visitors to its website choose materials and colors to customize their Air Force One shoes. In the next decade, the company expanded the service, called NIKEiD, to other types of apparel, adding design features and software, and setting up physical branches where customers can use the same tools and consult with designers. The latest twist is a feature called NIKE PHOTOiD that lets you send the company an image from your phone. Nike software then analyzes the colors in the photo, designs a shoe using those tints, and sends the design back to your phone with a click-to-purchase option.

On August 17, 1896, at the Crystal Palace in London, a forty-five-year-old woman by the name of Bridget Driscoll was supposedly the first fatality of an automobile accident in history. As she attempted to cross the grounds, a car struck her at a speed witnesses described as "a reckless pace, in fact, like a fire engine," so that she had no chance of reacting in time and getting out of its way.

Ironically, the car that hit her was moving "recklessly" at only four miles per hour (6 km/h), which is no faster than a walking pace. Yet at that time,

Bridgette Driscol 1896

this seemed positively out of control. Furthermore, the official investigation report of the accident proclaimed the sincere hope that no such accidents would ever happen again.

Obviously we have come a long way since then. At the turn of the nineteenth century, cars were still regarded as noisy, hazardous toys of the rich and in no way a threat to replace the horse and buggy as the primary means of transportation. The radical shift of their potential utility came about on the heels of visionary business pioneers. Some were predisposing, such as John D. Rockefeller, who realized that kerosene could replace whale oil as a better, cheaper, and cleaner source of fuel. He founded the Standard Oil Company in 1870, a precursor to Exxon Mobil and to a nationwide gasoline distribution infrastructure. And some pioneers were seminal, such as Henry Ford, who created a legitimate, lifestyle-enriching offering in 1908 with the Model T.

So how can you create legitimate lifestyle or workstyle enrichment in a fast-changing, continuously evolving environment in order to achieve ongoing relevance? **You have to be bold enough to be market driving rather than market driven.** Being market driven is no longer enough. You need to create your own market space that offers compellingly new enrichment to consumers rather than trying to react to your unpredictable and elusive environment. The audacious perspective of a market driver is summed up perfectly by the Henry Ford quote I mentioned earlier: "If I'd asked the consumer what they wanted, they'd have said a faster horse."

Nokia is a company that's market driving. Few people outside of Finland realize that Nokia is nearly 150 years old, and in its past the company has produced such diverse offerings as rifles, umbrellas, rubber boots, raincoats, tires, paper, and consumer electronics. Clearly the company has not identified itself as the provider of certain products but rather the provider of relevant products.

A monumental test to the company's survival came in 1991. Almost overnight, Nokia's biggest market ceased to exist when the Soviet Union dissolved as an economic entity. Imagine what you would do if you woke up one morning and found that your biggest market, your largest consumer base, had vanished. Could you even survive this kind of nightmare? Or, by shifting your perspective could you somehow use the calamity to quickly reorient your business toward even greater success? If so, how would you go about it?

As it happened, Nokia not only survived but thrived like never before—because it dared to be market driving. In 1991, its mobile phone unit was a small, peripheral division, yet the company recognized its potential as the driver of future growth. By 1994 Nokia sold off its industrial divisions and was listed on the New York Stock Exchange as the world's premier supplier of mobile phones, creating and driving a new market that it still dominates today. And by dominate, I mean that Nokia's share of the global cell phone market is greater than the combined market share of its top three competitors. It is also interesting to note that Nokia did not invent mobile phones. The first portable phone was developed in 1973 by Motorola. But as with the automobile, it took visionary thinking, in this case eighteen years later and by a company facing a severe test of survival, to give it life-enriching relevance for consumers.

Warning: Wireless connectivity not included!

Let's pause to fully absorb the profound prevalence of mobile phones that Nokia was instrumental in unleashing. Take a guess: how many cell phones do you think there are in the world today?

Think about it for a moment. Remember, we're talking about a product that did not exist in the public consciousness a mere twenty years ago. What's your answer?

An article in the *New York Times* reported in April 2010: "The number of mobile subscriptions in the world is expected to pass five billion this year, according to the International Telecommunication Union, a trade group. That would mean more human beings today have access to a cell phone than the United Nations says have access to a clean toilet."

Besides the omnipresence of mobile phones, another noteworthy phenomenon is that they are no longer primarily voice communication devices. In other words an industry created twenty years ago and adopted by an overwhelming portion of the world's population has already metamorphosed to such an extent that its core utility has been replaced. There is not a moment to stand still. In May 2010, the *New York Times* noted: "For the first time in the United States, the amount of data in text, e-mail messages, streaming video, music and other services on mobile devices in 2009 surpassed the amount of voice data in cell phone calls, industry executives and analysts say."

In essence, what we are seeing is an industry on steroids. In less than twenty years, mobile communication went from market introduction (challenging the conventional wisdom that phoning was tied to a fixed location), market acceptance, market saturation, market convergence, and market transformation. During this span, mobile phones became the convergence point for a myriad of traditionally separate industries, among them telecom, Internet, messaging, television, music, photography, news, market intelligence, gaming, banking, security, and navigation—which all drove their core functionality be expanded and then supplanted. In such an environment, can anyone afford not to be market driving?

Of course when you are the dominant industry player, everyone is out to get you. Nokia's competitors are gaining momentum. Apple's iPhone is capturing a formidable following and the number of Android devices activated each day continues to rise. Nokia's reign is continuously being challenged and will eventually end—unless it can continue to redefine its business to stay indispensably relevant to consumers. So what is Nokia's next frontier? Not surprisingly, something even more bold: Nokia wants to become a key driver of mobile experiences, not just its communication platform provider. Nokia sees the rapid convergence of both content and platforms and a wild race among visionary companies from diverse market segments to become the most indispensable source of mobile experiences of the future for consumers. And naturally it wants to be at the forefront of it—or risk being left behind in a sea of obsolescence. Its ambitions are pure market-driving stuff.

Here is another instance of a company clearly looking to be the market-driving enabler of a lifestyle trend that may very well become too irresistible to ignore. It came from the AFP newswires in March 2008:

> *German holidaymakers will be able to indulge their love of nudism by taking to the skies nude on special flights being launched this year, a travel company said on Monday.*
>
> *"In the former East Germany, naturist holidays were a much-loved way of spending the best weeks of the year," said the founder of OssiUrlaub.de, Enrico Hess.*
>
> *"We want to make that freedom possible above the clouds too," he said.*
>
> *"All the passengers will fly naked, but they are only allowed to undress once they are in the plane.*

But then they will be able to enjoy the hour-long flight in the way God intended," Hess said.

The pilot and the flight attendants will, however, keep their clothes on.

The first nude flights will be a day-trip on July 5 between Erfurt in southeast Germany and the Baltic Sea island of Usedom, which is fringed by white sand beaches.

Tickets cost 499 euros (735 dollars) and there are just 50 seats on board the jet.

What? A mere fifty seats per flight? Such glaring lack of sufficient capacity could cause a veritable stampede among potential passengers as this forward-looking offering just might ignite mass appeal among liberation-seeking consumers.

When talking about driving lifestyle trends, Starbucks is surely one of the most visible success stories of the past couple of decades. Here is a company that did not invent anything profound. Rather, it mimicked and repackaged. Starbucks adopted the social café concept, whose roots extend back to the Ottoman Empire of the sixteenth century, then became popular throughout Europe in the seventeenth century, and has been thriving there since. Starbucks molded and combined this concept with an efficient and replicable quick-service platform that allowed it to grow quickly and to provide a consistent experience all across the United States and then abroad. In doing so, Starbucks became one of the most recognized brands, acquired a fanatical (some even say addicted) following, and has grown into a $10 billion business.

Starbucks is a great example of fabricating compelling lifestyle enrichment by successfully combining already existing yet previously separate elements, rather than creating something that hasn't existed before, such as iTunes. **There is an exciting shortcut to becoming market driving: you don't necessarily have to invent something completely new; instead you can repackage already existing components in a meaningful, new way.** Having done the latter, Starbucks' lifestyle impact was profound. It changed the perception of coffee from being an enabler to being a destination, so rather than people taking their coffee to work (enabling them to be more alert), they are now taking work to their coffee (bringing laptops and conducting meetings at the cafés). In an increasingly disjointed society, coffee (of all things) has become a catalyst for people to stay connected, making cafés once again the pivotal social hubs that they were for centuries past—in large part due to Starbucks' pioneering lead.

If we take a step back, there is another, more generally applicable and thought-provoking meaning to this observation: in an increasingly disjointed society, consumers may find lifestyle-enriching comfort in offerings that retain elements of a more simple and harmonious past, much like they find increased comfort in gold or in religion during times of uncertainty. In this case, that anchor of familiarity is the café culture cloaked in contemporary flare.

What has amazed me most about Starbucks is not its proliferation in all the rural or less-spirited urban areas that were understandably void of social destinations, but rather its introduction and subsequent popularity in the heart of major cities that already enjoyed sophisticated café cultures. In Manhattan, for example, there seems to be a high-traffic Starbucks every few blocks, crowding out the local cafés. Even in Vienna, one of the cultural capitals of Europe, I visited a Starbucks in the center of the city that was overflowing with tourists and locals alike. Love it or hate it, you can't deny the success of the company's inventive market-driving strategy.

Finally, consider Amazon.com. This is a company that soared in annual revenues from $4 billion in 2002 to nearly $20 billion in 2008. What is the philosophy that enabled such growth? "If you want to continuously revitalize the service that you offer to your customers, you cannot stop at what you are good at," Amazon CEO Jeff Bezos told *BusinessWeek*. "You have to ask what your customers need and want, and then, no matter how hard it is, you better get good at those things."

When you ask such questions regarding consumer relevance continuously and intensely enough as an organization, you will start to infatuate consumers to the extent that they will recognize you as one of their favorite brands, and willingly follow you across market segments. Just look at the progression of Amazon. First, it was selling new books online, then the company expanded to providing a marketplace for used books, then all kinds of consumer goods, and in 2007, Amazon jumped from the services platform to a product-service hybrid with the Kindle e-book reader. Along the way Amazon has been transforming the very essence of the book industry as well as its own business in pursuit of the most broadly relevant consumer offerings and lifestyle enrichment.

What are the overall takeaways in terms of strategy and business application?

1 In order to infatuate, strive to be the provider of your consumers' favorite offering. Once you achieve that, you have a hold on their attention and affection and can widen your offering palette across market spaces and industries through a brand tied to your central offering.

2 Consumers have a capacity to form only a limited number of close, emotional associations with brands and offerings from among all those they come into contact with. You want to make sure that yours is one of them.

3 The way to achieve that is to think of yourself as being in the business of providing lifestyle enrichment to consumers. This perspective allows you to stay continuously relevant to a broad audience.

4 By watching children, you can observe their total immersion in, as well as fabrication of, meaningful experiences. These observations can help to pinpoint ways you can make your offering more enriching for consumers.

5 For B2B or heavy manufacturing businesses, the concept of lifestyle and workstyle enrichment has multifaceted applications. You should consider all of these in order to broaden your strategic possibilities.

6 Being relevant is more important than being best or being biggest. Counterintuitive to such managerial concepts as relative market share or operational excellence, it is not enough to have an efficient organization or to be the biggest or best within a traditional market segment. Instead, you need to continuously scan the horizon and shift course to stay relevant. In fact, being biggest or best may be a hindrance, because it impedes your ability and inclination to adapt quickly.

7 In order to stay relevant in a fast and continuously changing environment, you need to be market driving rather than market driven. Market driven, no matter how responsive, is a reactionary stance. In contrast, market driving is proactive, creating spaces of lifestyle enrichment that did not exist before.

8 As you set forth on being market driving and creating lifestyle enrichment for consumers, you must continuously monitor their reaction to and interaction with your offering. This allows you to validate the actual infatuation level of consumers and the length of each infatuation interval you create. Because, ideally, while you don't want to allow your consumers to slip out of the Infatuation Interval, you also don't want to introduce new extensions too early, while their current infatuation is still going strong. That would be wasteful and potentially confusing for consumers. Instead, you want to ride each Infatuation Interval as long as you can and jump to the next shortly before it's getting close to dissipating.

9 By nature of being market driving, you are shaping and molding the lifestyle of consumers, which needs to be done in a way that is easily understood, accepted, and embraced by them. The seamless integration of each innovation within the life of consumers is your goal, as summarized poignantly by Virginia

Postrel, a social trend commentator: "The most successful innovations are the ones that we stop noticing almost immediately."

So far I have suggested that it is human nature to be insatiable as consumers, which should inspire any business to continuously innovate. Businesses should aim to infatuate consumers and keep them infatuated by daring to be market driving, which is the basis for continuous relevance and lifestyle-enriching offerings. In the next chapter, we'll look at the indispensable ingredient of unconventional thinking in our quest to be market driving.

By EmmaBurnS

The Slingshot Framework

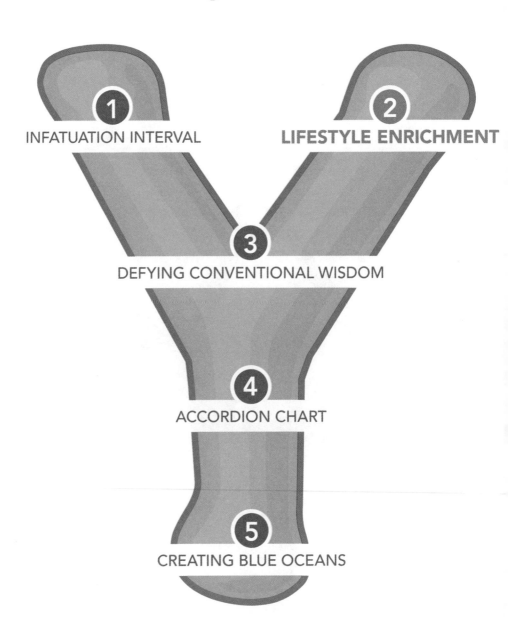

Have you visited **www.slingshotliving.com** lately?
If not, you're missing half the fun and learning.

DEFYING CONVENTIONAL WISDOM 3

I like nonsense, it wakes up the brain cells. Fantasy is a necessary ingredient in living. It's a way of looking at life through the wrong end of a telescope. Which is what I do. And that enables you to laugh at life's realities.

—Dr. Seuss, American author and illustrator (1904–91)

It may be hard to believe, but all of us were children once. As children, we all experienced the sense of elation and accomplishment from inventing our own games and making use of random props and terrain to choreograph a customized pastime that was a blast to play. There was virtually no limit to what we could play and where. What if we could reignite our childhood creativity and deconstruct our realm of acquired assumptions in the process? It would not only be disarmingly fun but deeply meaningful in guiding our strategic thinking.

Here is the connection: the basis of the most successful strategies is not outcompeting rivals, but rather creating your own game, your own market space. This approach is especially important during turbulent times, when traditional market definitions and standards disappear.

There is a growing recognition that creativity—or resourcefulness, as I like to re-label it—is a vital component for successfully handling unexpected, unprecedented, and rapidly changing surroundings. As an example, the *Bloomberg Businessweek* article "What Chief Executives Really Want," in May 2010, noted: "According to a new survey of 1,500 chief executives conducted by IBM's Institute for Business Value, CEOs identify 'creativity' as the most important leadership competency for the successful enterprise of the future." Think about this for a moment. Of all personal qualities, business leaders picked creativity as the key foundation for future success, ahead of such traditional pillars as operational expertise, industry know-how, interpersonal skills, or even innovation. How fascinating. There is clearly a mind-set shift in motion, which leads to the question: If creativity is thrust to the forefront of vital leadership qualities, how can you fully embrace it? How can you tap into your personal reservoir of resourceful thinking?

I spent my childhood in Budapest, Hungary, which at the time was part of the Eastern bloc of Communist countries. I grew up in the heart of the city. One time, in the early 1970s, when I was eight or nine years old, I was visiting my best friend at his family's apartment. It was early winter, and we were both itching to do something new, fun, and slightly mischievous. But how could we? We had nothing at our disposal except bland, everyday things and our imagination. So we improvised a pastime out of the ordinary things that surrounded us. Armed only with a few random household items—a matchbox, sugar cubes, some sticky tape, and a bit of string—we invented a game in a matter of minutes.

It went like this: my friend's family lived in an apartment above a popular home-furnishing store on a busy street. The apartment had a balcony perched over the prominent front store window where pedestrians would stop and eye the displays. So we took the empty matchbox, stuffed it with a few sugar cubes for added

My personal shrine to childhood ingenuity: The very place in the center of Budapest where my story took place. Amazingly, its ambiance has changed little over thirty years. See if you can find it the next time you visit the city.

weight, and wrapped it in outward-facing sticky tape. We lowered the sticky contraption from the balcony using some string, carefully maneuvering it to land unnoticeably on top of the winter hat of a window shopper below. Then came the pinnacle moment. We briskly yanked on the string, which caused the hat to momentarily lift off the person's head. We did this urban catch-and-release routine over and over as new people shuffled by the store window, and we thought the startled reaction and colorful cursing of our victims was the funniest thing in the world.

It was pure, untainted fun. At the time we knew that this game was completely our own. We invented it and perfected it. It was empowering and exhilarating. To this day, over three decades later, my friend and I still reminisce about it, etched in our memory as a highlight of our youth and a symbol of our former resourcefulness.

What does this story remind you of from your childhood? What game did you invent that brings back fond memories? All of us have stories like this that bubble to the surface when properly triggered. They may be deeply buried, but they are recoverable. And you should recover them, because they will help to make you a more successful and more balanced adult. Unfortunately, the tendency as we grow older is to put aside childish things, including our sense of continuous exploration and invention. Our imagination gives way to conformity, fun cedes to seriousness. **So the first step in uncovering your buried slingshot—the symbol of your dormant childhood creativity—is to evoke a sufficient catalyst and framework.** Which is exactly what we are after here.

I have a challenge for you. No matter where you happen to be reading this book, be it in your home, your office, in a restaurant, a garden, on an airplane, or somewhere else, take a quick look around you. Absorb the various mundane things that you see. Now try to fabricate a game or a sport using them as props. These are all things you see every day in the same way and don't give much thought to. But now let your imagination take over and see them as objects of fun. Look to my story above as your guide. Go!

How did you do? How long did it take you to come up with something? Moreover, do you think that your game would be fun to try? Did you find the exploratory process of this exercise difficult? Did you find it meaningful? In essence, this simple exercise represents exactly the thinking process that we need to reclaim, that came so naturally when we were children. I can reposition the challenge this way: take a look at the familiar resources of your business or the characteristics of your personal environment that surround you. **Now think of new applications, new combinations, new angles that would allow you to overstep perceived limitations of your business or your environment in a way that provides new levels of enrichment. By doing so, nothing has changed, except your perspective and the boundary lines of your imagination.** Which in turn serves to unlock meaningful new possibilities.

Here are a few of my favorite invented games that make use of ordinary objects and surroundings:

Balloon-Couch Volleyball: This sport is a variation of volleyball and can be played in most any family home. It makes use of two everyday objects in an unexpected combination: a balloon and a couch. Rules: two teams face each other on opposite sides of a couch (front and back) and hit the balloon back and forth, trying to make it touch the floor on the other team's side before anyone from the other team can get to it. Any body part can be used to hit the balloon or to save it from falling to the floor. Each team has three touches to get the balloon over the couch. The couch itself is neutral, meaning that the balloon is allowed to bounce off it. The balloon's lightness makes the game both harmless to the surroundings and a blast to play.

Saltshaker Curling: This sport is a variation of the Winter Olympic sport of curling, where players from two teams slide round objects on the ice, trying to get them to stop within a circular target area. Saltshaker Curling brings together two ordinary objects in an unconventional way: a kitchen table and a tabletop saltshaker. Rules: two players, seated at opposite sides, take turns sliding the saltshaker toward the other side of the table, trying to make it stop as close to the edge as possible without falling off. The game goes on for twenty attempts each. Once players get good, the winner often gets the shaker to stop where it partially hangs over the edge of the table without falling off.

Speed Leaf-Catching: This is a very simple but exhilarating outdoor game. It requires only one common object: an autumn tree with falling leaves. Rules: players position themselves around the tree, and they try to catch as many falling leaves as possible before they hit the ground. The game is played for five minutes. The winner is the person who grabs the most leaves.

How about it? Are you motivated to try one of these games or perhaps create your own variation? If you need a bit more inspiration, try this: whenever you have the opportunity, give children some random objects, ask them to make up a game, and watch them play. Observe how they think, how they relate to the objects and to each other. Learn and be inspired.

"To be successful we must live from our imaginations, not from our memories."
—Stephen Covey, author and leadership expert

Another thing I encourage you to do is to honor the one publicly recognized, annual celebration of childish frolic: April Fools' Day. What a great concept. The first of April is the one day every year when adults have full license to be impish and playful. The act of planning and executing a ruse helps to reconnect you with your inner child, so take advantage of it. The best April Fools' pranks are not unkind or nasty, nor are they designed to mock but rather to challenge your perception of reality and the limits of conventionality. What is absurd and what is sensible? How can these artificial boundaries be overstepped or even reversed through a hoax? You should partake in reality-bending April Fools' activities and encourage those you work with to do the same. It is liberating and opens up channels of unconventional thinking.

The process of coming up with the appropriate setting and choreography for a prank that tests people's reality frontiers is in itself therapeutic. For example, I find scuba diving a superb backdrop for a practical joke. When a diver is submerged, he is completely cut off from the world, and his sense of reality can be viably challenged. A possible scheme could go like this: Divers are ferried by boat to an offshore dive site and proceed to take the plunge as planned. While they are below, the dive boat races out of view and is replaced with a replica of an ancient Roman vessel, with a crew in period costumes. When the divers ascend to the surface, the Romans, speaking only Latin, act very astonished and quite scared of them. Reluctantly they allow the divers to climb onto the craft, but being from many centuries ago,

their misunderstandings continue to mount. Just as the divers are beginning to question their own perception of reality, a crewman whips out a mobile phone and a WaveRunner is prompted to race by, exposing the joke.

Here is another farcical scenario. Take a stretch of an imposing five-lane highway and make it innocuously merge into four lanes. Repeat the lane reduction at short intervals, until only a single lane remains. Then gradually shift the road surface from asphalt to dirt, and finally phase out the road incrementally altogether, leaving drivers in the middle of nowhere. Such an experiment would test the rigidity of people's adherence to the assumption that all roads must lead to somewhere.

These kinds of comic situations that unexpectedly nudge people out of their comfort zone were elevated to an art form by the legendary Allen Funt through his seminal reality television show *Candid Camera*, which started way back in 1948. More recently, and in a more extreme fashion, Ashton Kutcher in the MTV show *Punk'd* followed in Funt's footsteps. Although Kutcher tended to go a bit too far, his pranks nevertheless expose how quickly our sense of normalcy can be challenged and how seriously we take ourselves. What's more, watching such situational musings brings you to confront the question of how you would react if you were suddenly thrust into a circumstance that seems downright absurd and illogical. Kind of like the one that Nokia executives faced in 1991, when overnight the company's biggest market (the Soviet Union) ceased to exist. Or the situation Kodak executives were

confronted with in 2003 when their long-standing core business of film photography suddenly seemed irrelevant with the advent of digital photography. Could you keep your cool in such a scenario? Would you have the mental flexibility to take control of the situation? I encourage you to catch a rerun or two of *Punk'd* to fuel your thinking.

Let's turn to a real-life illustration of injecting some humor into the workplace. A European bank recently held a company-wide weekend event at a countryside hotel as a token of appreciation to its employees. Unbeknown to the bank's top executives, but with their tacit consent, the organizers orchestrated a practical joke on them. Phony policemen flagged down each senior manager one by one on the highway leading to the hotel, scolded them for reckless driving, and issued them traffic violations. Because the charges were bogus, the incidents were filmed by a hidden camera to capture the indignant reactions of the executives. The resulting humorous footage was played on a large screen in front of the bank's entire staff at the hotel. What do you think is the effect of something like this? It sends a message that fun is allowed in the organization, and even top executives are not immune to laughing at themselves and allowing others to do the same. It builds a company-wide emotional alignment and a foundation for open, creative expression, enriching the workstyle experience of employees. In turn, more content and more engaged employees serve to make the bank itself more successful.

In the last chapter, I will describe in detail a self-originated entertainment-media platform whose purpose is to help reignite our youthful sense of limitless exploration and fun. It's called Team-O Entertainment and is based on the principles of the mysterious yet seemingly highly influential Federation of Oxymoronic Sports.

There was once a boy whose mind would freely wander and who had difficulty concentrating when in school. As a result, after just three months of formal education, he was labeled a problem child and was pulled out by his mother who thought otherwise. He became homeschooled. Along the way he discovered his passion for science, conducted experiments, and started creating various inventions. That boy went on to own over a thousand patents and brought to the world, among other things, the phonograph, the light bulb, the motion picture camera, the typewriter, and central power stations that could provide electricity to multiple users. The latter became the foundation for his company, now known as General Electric. When *Life* magazine ranked the one hundred most influential people of the last millennium, he was chosen as the single most important person in the entire world over the past one thousand years and given the label Man of the Millennium. That boy was Thomas Edison.

On one occasion, he was asked by a reporter, "Mr. Edison, you being the greatest inventor in the world, what do you consider the greatest invention?" Edison replied without hesitation: "The mind of a child."

How many times have you heard adults say, or said yourself, such things as, "I wish I was a child again," or "Deep down, I am still just a child." What is the meaning of such declarations? They are expressing not just a longing but also an acceptance of the notion that being childlike is unseemly for grown-ups, that we are either one or the other but not both. Are they not? In contrast, my contention is that there ought to be no artificial repression but rather a full embrace and liberation of our youthful spirit, which Thomas Edison labeled as the greatest invention of all.

In 1988, a highly popular, multiple Academy Award–nominated movie hit the screens. It was entitled *Big* and starred Tom Hanks playing a twelve-year-old boy named Josh whose wish of becoming an adult is suddenly granted by a fortune-teller contraption at an amusement park. Since he remains a twelve-year-old on the inside, he is able to penetrate the adult world while retaining his childish perspective. The resulting contrast is both humorously entertaining and poignant. An online movie database says, "The real beauty of the movie lies in the realization that an adult that manages to maintain the innocence and exuberance of youth is one to be greatly envied."

As the plot unfolds, Josh gets a job at a toy manufacturing company, where out-of-touch adults are trying to conceptualize new toys that children would find fun and meaningful. Of course, their inherent rigidity makes this a near impossible task. In contrast, Josh is able to offer simple, consequential insights, and along with his infectiously playful personality, he quickly rises within the company ranks. One of the most memorable scenes of the film is when Josh inspires the company's elderly owner to jump on and play a duet with him on a giant foot-operated electronic keyboard at FAO Schwarz, the famous toy store in New York City.

As I said, given the right stimulus, everyone—regardless of age—can be nudged to rediscover their childhood creativity. Allow yourself to be nudged. In Appendix B, I include some tips, an activity, and a timeless toy which will enable you to reclaim your playfulness.

"A business has to be involving, it has to be fun, and it has to exercise your creative instincts."
—Sir Richard Branson, founder and
chairman of Virgin Group

By letting their imaginations reign, what children excel at is unrestrained, unconventional thinking. It is this very ability to challenge conventional wisdom, to think in a counterintuitive manner, that can enable businesses to be market driving, to deliver life-style enrichment and repeated infatuations of consumers. Let's explore the power of unconventional thinking more deeply.

A 2009 article in the *St. Petersburg Times* reported: "Steve Forbes, editor-in-chief of *Forbes* magazine, was browsing in a Florida bookstore a few years ago when he picked up a copy of *Hannibal Crosses the Alps* by Eckerd College classics professor John Prevas. As he reviewed the book for his magazine, Forbes was struck by two things: that the elements of successful leadership have not changed in 2,000 years and that anyone who accomplishes something great or unique, whether in business or politics, often does so by defying conventional wisdom. Forbes contacted Prevas, and the two collaborated on a book that came out in the summer of 2009, entitled: *Power Ambition Glory: The Stunning Parallels Between Great Leaders of the Ancient World and Today—and the Lessons You Can Learn.* Among the ancient leaders profiled are the famous—Julius Caesar and Alexander the Great—and lesser-knowns like Xenophon, who emerged from nowhere at a time of crisis to lead a defeated and demoralized Greek army out of Persia."

That is a rather powerful and provocative observation by Steve Forbes: "Anyone who accomplishes something great or unique, whether in business or politics, often does so by defying conventional wisdom." But if you think about it, it seems perfectly true and accurate. Just imagine how profoundly different our world might be today if the American Founding Fathers didn't have the vision and audacity to create an entirely new model of government based on the unalienable rights to life, liberty, and the pursuit of happiness and on the principle of checks and balances. Now look back in history and think of your favorite examples. Here are a couple of mine.

In the eleventh and twelfth centuries BC, one of the great epic wars of ancient times was fought. The Greeks assembled a massive flotilla of warships and brought its might against the city of Troy. Their mission was to take back Helen, the outrageously abducted Greek queen, and to punish the Trojans for the fiendish act. But the city had formidable defenses, and the two armies remained deadlocked. There they stood, shield to shield, lance to lance, neither able to budge the other. The siege went on like this for ten fruitless years.

Then the Greeks had an idea that changed everything. The Greek army pretended to dissolve camp and sail away. They left behind a large wooden horse, which the Trojans mistook as a token of peace. They dragged it inside the city walls and began to celebrate. Little did they suspect that under the cover of night a handful of enemy soldiers hiding inside the statue would emerge

to pry open the city's gates for the rest of the Greek army, which had circled back in full force. Once inside, the Greeks won the battle quickly and decisively against the utterly surprised and unprepared Trojans.

Were the Greeks cheaters? Or did they simply overstep taken-for-granted assumptions of warfare? By changing the rules of conduct and expanding the boundaries of engagement—much like David did against Goliath—the Greeks defied conventional wisdom and achieved one of the most famous victories in history. In the process, the Trojan horse ended the conflict swiftly, minimizing the cost of victory in terms of effort, time, and number of lives lost on both sides.

Let's return for a moment to Florence, Italy, where the famous statue of David stands. The crowning jewel of the city's medieval architecture is the towering Cathedral of Santa Maria del Fiora, better known as the Duomo. Much like Michelangelo's *David*, the Duomo is also a symbol of flouting conventionality. Fodor's guidebook to Florence, Tuscany, and Umbria observed:

It was to be the largest dome in the world, surpassing Rome's Pantheon. But when the time finally came to build the dome in 1418, no one was sure how—or even if—it could be done. Florence was faced with a 143-ft (44 m) hole in the roof of its cathedral, and one of the greatest challenges in the history of architecture.

Fortunately, local genius Filippo Brunelleschi was just the man for the job. Brunelleschi won the competition to design the dome, and for the next 18 years he oversaw its construction. The enormity of his achievement can hardly be overstated. Working on such a large scale required him to invent hoists and cranes that were engineering marvels. Perhaps most remarkably, he executed the construction without a supporting wooden framework, which has previously been thought indispensable.

And how about a story from the medical world, which I learned as a schoolboy in Budapest? It is not only an illustration of unconventional thinking but also serves to highlight the often prevalent resistance to new ideas. In the mid-nineteenth century, mortality rates among women giving birth were terribly high in Europe, oscillating between 10 and 35 percent, primarily due to puerperal fever (childbed fever). In 1847, Ignac Semmelweis, a twenty-nine-year-old Hungarian physician working at a hospital in Vienna, noticed that the doctors' ward had three times the mortality rate of the ward run by midwives. Intrigued and determined, his inquiry led him to a deceptively simple explanation: because of their multitasking with diverse patients and even cadavers, doctors' hands were the carriers of infectious disease, and therefore needed to be washed before handling births. Once his suggestion was instituted, the hospital's mortality rate dropped from 18 to 1 percent!

But that was not enough to convince his contemporaries. Even though Semmelweis is now considered a medical pioneer and the "savior of mothers", his peers rejected his findings for their sheer simplicity and inconsistency with prevailing views of disease. The Wikipedia article on Semmelweis notes: "The so-called Semmelweis reflex or effect is a metaphor for a certain type of human behavior characterized by reflex-like rejection of new knowledge because it contradicts entrenched norms, beliefs or para-digms—named after Semmelweis whose perfectly reasonable hand-washing suggestions were ridiculed and rejected by his contemporaries."

Ignac Semmelweis as a child

I could not help but think of the Semmelweis reflex when the Wii first came out in 2006. Initial reviews by gaming industry experts chided Nintendo for bring-ing to market a product whose graphics and display quality looked amateurish. Of course, they were passing judg-ment on the Wii based on tradi-tional industry standards and could not grasp the transformative power of Nintendo's unconventional strategy: to deemphasize graphics and display quality in favor of active sports simulation—a previously unprec-edented take on video games. How could these early critics have guessed that the Wii's seeming amateurishness was a guise for an ingenious industry innovation that would unlock appeal for video games across all consumer demographics?

If you want a rousing illustration of challenging conventional wisdom from the realm of politics, how about this: In 1961, President John F. Kennedy boldly asserted that the United States would put a man on the moon before the end of the decade. He proclaimed: "I believe that this nation should commit itself to achieving the goal, before this decade is out, of landing a man on the Moon and returning him safely to the Earth. No single space project in this period will be more impressive to mankind, or more important in the long-range exploration of space; and none will be so difficult or expensive to accomplish."

Was President Kennedy delusional? Did he not realize that his statement was illogical, that it had no basis in reality? At the time of his speech, only one American had flown in space (less than a month earlier), NASA had not yet sent a man into orbit, and the technological basis for orchestrating such a mission did not yet exist. Even some NASA employees doubted the feasibility of this ambitious goal. Meeting President Kennedy's challenge required a remarkable flurry of technological creativity. And guess what? America delivered. *Apollo 11* landed on the moon on July 20, 1969, as the whole world held its breath in amazement, and Neil Armstrong and Buzz Aldrin became the first men to set foot on it.

Daring to dream big and setting ambitious, seemingly impossible goals are what some of the greatest men in history have done and what visionary business leaders do. Their vision inspires their team to be highly creative, because the targeted goals cannot be met by traditional means. As Kevin Rollins, former CEO of Dell, expressed it in 2004 at the height of the company's success: "I set irrational goals (Michael [Dell] and I together), to encourage our team so they don't think of conventional solutions. If we asked for a 10 or 20 percent increase in productivity, we'd get conventional solutions. But if we ask them to double their productivity, then they have to rethink everything."

Coincidentally, there is a concept in space exploration called gravitational slingshot, which is the use of the relative movement and gravity of a planet or other celestial bodies to alter the path and speed of a spacecraft, typically in order to save fuel, time, and expense. The *Mariner 10* probe was the first spacecraft to use the gravitational slingshot effect to reach another planet, slinging past Venus on February 5, 1974, in order to explore Mercury for the first time. Using the gravitational pull of planets to propel spacecraft? Now that seems like a brilliantly novel and unconventional concept!

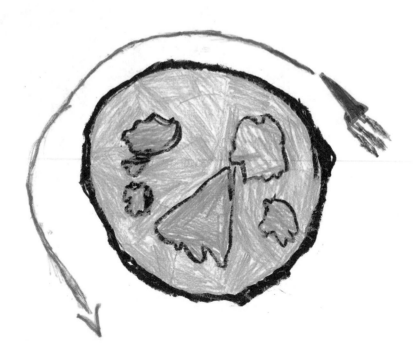

Another example from very recent history revolves around the recipients of the 2006 Nobel Peace Prize, awarded to Muhammad Yunus and to Grameen Bank, which Yunus founded in Bangladesh. As a pioneer in the arena of social capitalism, Yunus showed that good business and social benevolence, which are traditionally pursued separately, can be successfully combined. Grameen Bank demonstrated the profound social impact and strong financial viability of microlending by providing loans to the poorest of the poor in rural Bangladesh without any collateral—an idea that defies conventional logic. According to Muhammad Yunus, "If it's not profitable, it's not microlending—it's charity." His long-term vision is to eliminate poverty in the world, and Grameen Bank has been turning this lofty vision into practical reality. Based on the bank's model of microlending, millions of underprivileged people around the world are rising from poverty, not as a result of charity, but as a result of good business. How is that for a powerful, seemingly incompatible combination?

As you read these stirring examples, how do you reflect on your business? What new ideas do they kindle in you?

Another arena with great stories about defying conventional wisdom and with rich parallels to business strategy is the world of sports. Let's look at just a few.

In 1954, Englishman Roger Bannister became the first person ever to run a mile in less than four minutes. Breaking this barrier had mythical connotations, because before his accomplishment, the prevailing wisdom was that the human body was simply not designed to run that fast. But the fascinating thing was that within ten years after his run, over three hundred others also ran the mile in under four minutes. What does this tell you? It shows that

the four-minute barrier was not a physiological but a psychological one, and all it took was one person to prove that overstepping it was possible. Similarly, many of the barriers that surround businesses and limit their strategic possibilities exist only in the minds of managers and executives, who just need to be bold enough to overstep them.

Then there are some colorful examples from American football, which is a furious game of strategy. In fact it is so strategy intensive, that the game is paused for half a minute between each play to allow both teams to formulate or select the best strategy for the next one. Believe it or not, there are now headsets inside players' helmets so that coaches can quickly relay commands between plays from the sidelines. For the uninitiated, the game can look downright disjointed or ridiculously drawn out, but in fact it is designed to allow for the right balance of thinking, planning, and action. What fans are treated to in each game is the repeated combination of rapid strategy formation and execution.

With that said, do you know the year and the score of the most one-sided championship game in the history of professional American football? Think for a moment or take a guess. The answer is 1940 (well before the Super Bowl era, which began in 1967), when the Chicago Bears defeated the Washington Redskins by a score of 73–0. That is an absolute walloping. It's comparable to saying that Brazil once beat Germany 10–0 in the World Cup Final of European football. It's hard to believe. So why did it happen? How could one team beat another to such a degree when playing in the championship of any tightly contested sport? After all, you would not expect such a glaring disparity between the two best teams.

You don't really have to know the game to appreciate the answer. In its simplest terms, American football is played by two teams, each taking turns trying to get an elliptical ball from one end of the field to the other, with the other team trying to prevent it from doing so. Whichever team can do this more often, either by running or throwing and catching the ball, wins. So let me set the stage for this game. Back in 1940, three weeks prior to the championship game, the same two teams met in Chicago, and the Redskins were triumphant 7–3. This time the game was to be played in Washington, so naturally the Redskins were favored to win. Additionally, this was to be the first nationally broadcast game on the radio, so millions of people would be tuning in, adding to the hype.

What triggered such an unexpected and complete trouncing by the Bears? The answer is the T formation. This was the first time in the history of the sport that a team featured a new strategic formation—having two players who could potentially run with the ball. They stood behind and on either side of the quarterback, as in a letter *T*, hence the name. Why was this such a big deal? Traditionally, each team had only one single runner, or running back, so that the defense would know exactly who would get the ball and who they had to stop. But with the T formation, all of a sudden there were two potential running backs to stop, and there was no way to know which would get the ball. This seemingly simple, additional layer of flexibility was so potent that the Redskins were unable to put up any meaningful resistance.

Again the question arises, as with the Greeks in Troy, were the Bears cheating? Did they break any rules? Of course not! They simply challenged the taken-for-granted mode of engagement

and created their own variation of the game within the confines of the overall rules. By doing so, they no longer had to go head to head, strength to strength with a formidable opponent. Instead, they tweaked their strategy in a way that their opponent could not possibly anticipate or be prepared for (think again of David vs. Goliath). And here is the critical point in terms of business application: **When you overstep barriers and shed assumptions, you no longer have to be the best by any traditional measure.** It no longer mattered if the Bears had the single-best running back, as long as the Redskins had no idea which of two runners they needed to stop.

By virtue of creating their own version of the game via the T formation, the Bears became the best at it. In other words, they willingly forfeited to be best in the traditional sense in exchange for creating a new standard that made them best in a more relevant way. By being game changing or market driving, the Bears minimized the cost of victory (not trying to outduel the Redskins in conventional ways that they expected), while at the same time maximizing the margin of victory, *and* they provided exceptional, new value to consumers (as spectators and listeners were suddenly treated to a more entertaining, multifaceted game). Such combination of accomplishments is a central theme of Blue Ocean Strategy, which I will talk about in a later chapter.

To bring the example full circle back to the business world, some years ago I attended a luncheon where Klaus Kleinfeld (then CEO of Siemens USA, soon thereafter overall CEO of Siemens) opened a speech by referencing the very same story about the Bears-Redskins game. His message was that he wanted to inspire every employee within his massive organization to think of ways every day to be like the 1940 Bears, continuously scanning and overstepping boundaries in pursuit of providing new value to consumers and for the company.

A more recent and equally fascinating example from American football is that of Texas Tech University head football coach Mike Leach. Coach Leach was named the Collegiate Football Coach of the Year in 2008 and was widely recognized as revolutionizing the way American college football is being played, based on his coaching approach that defies conventional wisdom.

Texas Tech had nowhere near the resources of some of the great football universities in America. It lacked the prestige, funding, and reach to recruit the best athletes. So, in a traditional sense, Texas Tech would have no business in being among the best, yet it flirted with an undefeated season and was ranked as high as number two in the nation in 2008.

Not surprisingly, Coach Leach's approach was to sidestep the competition. He instituted a strategy that uses a so-called spread offense, meaning that he would have up to five players on the field who could catch the ball (receivers) instead of the standard two or three, and the team would try to pass the ball on almost every play instead of mixing in a lot of running plays. This unusual, unbalanced attack eventually wore down far bigger and stronger opponents, who were both confused and fatigued in trying to defend against it. The result was a string of successful and incredibly entertaining games. In December 2006, Texas Tech made college football history by posting the biggest comeback ever in a season finale.

On Rivals.com, Andrew Bagnato noted: "Trailing Minnesota by four touchdowns at halftime, Texas Tech coach Mike Leach told his team it had a chance to make history. The pep talk turned out to be a prediction. The Red Raiders spotted Minnesota a 31-point, third-quarter lead, then rallied for a stunning 44–41 overtime victory in the Insight Bowl Friday night, the largest comeback in Division I-A bowl history."

Coach Leach also had a special ability to get ordinary people to do extraordinary things—turning less-heralded recruits into star athletes, as well as finding unusual ways of identifying talent. One illustration is the story of when his team lacked a quality place kicker. Instead of taking the traditional recruiting route, Coach Leach invited student spectators during the halftime of a game to a kicking contest. The winner of the contest then became a kicker for the team.

Not altogether surprisingly, his unconventional style eventually became a point of contention with the university. After a decade of leadership during which he became the winningest coach in school history, Coach Leach was let go by Texas Tech in the wake of a procedural spat in December 2009.

Finally, let's reflect on the origins of some of the world's most popular sports, which is a nice way to tie the topic of unconventional thinking back to childhood playing. Legend has it that during a game of soccer in 1823, William Webb Ellis, a sixteen-year-old student at the Rugby School in England, caught the ball in a moment of spontaneous improvisation and started running with it toward the opponent's goal line. Thus the game of rugby was born. Running with the ball was officially allowed in 1841, and rugby went on to become the foundation for both American and Australian football.

What about the origin of basketball? This sport had an equally unusual, even oxymoronic beginning. Back in 1891, in the town of Springfield, Massachusetts, a young physical education teacher was frustrated by the unusually long and harsh winter, which prevented his students from going outdoors to exercise. He tried to fabricate indoor versions of both lacrosse and soccer, but neither was successful.

So he nailed a peach basket to the balcony at both ends of the school gym and defined the object of the game as throwing a soccer ball into the opposing team's basket. He divided the students into two teams and made up a few rules. Initially, the ball had to be retrieved from the baskets with the help of a ladder. Basket ball, as it was known back then, was thus conceived, and it went on to become one of the world's most popular sports—a game invented by combining formerly incompatible, common objects in a new way. Like we did all the time when we were kids. In this instance, an unusually harsh environment was the cradle of invention.

What examples of unconventional thinking can you cite from the world of sports? What fresh, unusual ideas might you have to make current sports more interesting to play or to watch? Here is one of mine: In all sporting events that are measured against time (such as running or swimming), the competition distances ought to be modified every two years. This would lead to much more frequent record settings and therefore make the sport more exciting for both participants and spectators. For example, the 400-meter run could be changed to 425 meters, then down to 380, etc. A similar variety can be introduced to other sports as well. Instead of a javelin all the time, why not see who could toss a beach umbrella the farthest? Or instead of a shot put, why not have athletes hurl a watermelon at the next Olympics?

I mentioned above that an unrelenting winter season was the backdrop for the invention of basketball. Which leads us to the question, What is the right strategy in a highly unpredictable or unfavorable environment? No doubt the world economic crisis, triggered by the meltdown of the U.S. housing finance market, suddenly brought everyone face to face with this question in 2008. The speed and scope by which the crisis spread across market segments and international borders was unprecedented. By its nature, such a calamity forces us to reexamine our business and to discard strategies based on environmental conditions that have been turned upside down. But this takes courage. Our natural instinct is to dig in and try to ride out the storm. Yet with a change in perspective, even a period of severe tempest can be seen as a time of great opportunities. SpicyIP.com points out: "After all, many of the world's enduring, multibillion-dollar corporations, from Disney to Microsoft, were founded during economic down-

turns. Generally speaking, operating costs tend to be cheaper in a recession. Talent is easier to find because of widespread layoffs. And competition is usually less fierce because, frankly, many players are taken out of the game."

Let's take a quick break and go on a skiing adventure together. Imagine doing a full day of intense skiing, and taking a chairlift up for the final run at the end of the afternoon. When you get off the lift, you find yourself at the top of a high mountain peak. It's getting dark and you are feeling tired. Suddenly it hits you that the only way back to the village below is to ski down the single steep slope, which is beyond your ability. As you start to ski down filled with fear and reluctance, your instinct tells you to lean back away from the precipitous drop in front of you. However, this stance has exactly the opposite, unwanted effect. It puts pressure on the back of your skis, accelerating you down the slope and out of control. What should you do instead? You need to lean forward and push your weight on the front of your skis, which allows for a controlled descent.

This same approach holds in business during periods of adversity. If out of fear your gut reaction is to recoil and to start cutting costs just to survive, your very actions may be choking off the growth of your business and accelerating its potential demise. But if you lean forward and embrace the challenge of adversity, you may find ways not only to survive but to prosper. Think back to the story of Nokia from the previous chapter. You can still cut costs or reallocate resources, but you do it in a way that has the strategic growth of your business in mind, not its mere survival. How to do this will be discussed in subsequent chapters.

Three Tourists and the Hungry Lion

Three tourists are on a safari in Africa. While they are walking along in a nature reserve, a ferocious lion suddenly jumps out of the bush in front of them. It is hungry and sees an opportunity to make an easy kill. It roars loudly, showing its fangs. Its intentions are clear: it wants to feast on one of the unlucky tourists.

The first tourist, terrified and overcome by fear, turns white, stops dead in his tracks, and is unable to move. The second tourist, after a moment of reflection, starts to shed all his unnecessary equipment and clothing and begins to stretch out. Meanwhile, the third tourist stands there with his hands in his pockets, calmly assessing the situation.

After a couple of seconds, the first tourist looks at the second and yells hysterically, "You're crazy! There is nothing you can do to outrun this lion!" The second tourist turns to him and says, "You are right, but it's not the lion that I have to outrun. It's one of the two of you." A couple of seconds later,

*the third tourist reaches into his pocket, pulls out a
lighter, flicks it on, and scares away the lion.*

What's the lesson of this story? To be sure, there are parallels
between this perilous encounter and the worrisome situation facing companies during periods of adversity. The three tourists represent the different reactions companies tend to have. The first,
of course, is the one that is completely caught off guard and is
unable to adjust, finding himself in the most vulnerable position.
The second tourist is a little bit better, but his strategy is merely
that of survival. His thinking is that he will be okay as long as he is
not the one caught by the lion, and his shedding of unnecessary
equipment is symbolic of companies slashing expenses just to stay
afloat. In contrast, the third tourist personifies the perspective of
defying conventional wisdom by which companies do not have to
accept the undesirable finality of a volatile situation. Instead, they
can look for creative alternatives that may be very simple, even
trivial, in hindsight. The third tourist puts himself in full control of
the situation by the simple, unexpected step of igniting a lighter.

"Some men see things as they are and say 'Why?'
I dream of things that never were and say 'Why not?'"
—George Bernard Shaw, Irish playwright (1856–1950)

So how can you begin to harness the power of unconventional thinking? I think it starts by looking at the world through an inquisitive, investigative lens, as you did as a child. And this perspective should not be limited just to your work, but it should permeate your general outlook on life. After all, some of the greatest inspirations and most profound unconventional ideas will come to you in moments and situations completely removed from your business. **The whole world is your reservoir for unconventional ideas.**

To whet your appetite, I offer a couple of personal observations on how common offerings today could be reinvented through unconventional thinking.

During a flight in 2007, I came across an interesting statistic in an issue of *Travel and Leisure* magazine: "Alaskan Airlines found that by removing just 5 magazines per aircraft, it could save $10,000 per year on fuel costs." This finding triggered my thinking on how airline frequent flyer programs could be and should be remodeled. Here is the thing: frequent flyer programs have two major flaws—they are all more or less identical, so there is no real differentiation or distinctive enrichment being offered, and they are not only seldom loved but often downright resented by both principal constituent groups. Travelers are suspicious of the programs because of the restrictive redemption rules and expiration schemes, and the airlines are wary because the programs represent accumulating liability against future profits by committing to provide more and more complimentary seats on future flights.

This is clearly a situation that is far from ideal, yet everyone seems to accept its current limitations as though they are unchangeable. Why does this have to be? What is needed is a way to align the interests of the airlines and the passengers and to create a more motivational system for both. But how? Let's return to the statistic above. If removing just a few magazines from an airplane can result in such a large cost savings in fuel, then surely an airplane's operating cost is very sensitive to the amount of weight it is carrying. In fact, as it turns out, the single largest expense of operating an airline is its fuel cost. According to an International Air Transport Association (IATA) economic briefing in June 2007: "For the first time ever, fuel replaced labor as the largest single cost item for the global airline industry in 2006. Based on a sample of the financial reports of 45 major global (passenger) airlines, fuel accounted for 25.5% of total operating costs in 2006."

> **"My principal business consists of giving commercial value to the brilliant, but misdirected, ideas of others.... Accordingly, I never pick up an item without thinking of how I might improve it."**
> —Thomas Edison, American inventor (1847–1931)

Let's get this straight. Fuel cost for airlines is the single largest expense, chewing up over a quarter of total operating costs. Airlines are scrambling to reduce the overall weight on flights by seemingly trifling means (such are removing in-flight magazines and blankets) in a desperate attempt to save fuel. Yet aside from the general limits on baggage dimension and weight and recent punitive charges for each piece of checked luggage, the airlines have done nothing to positively motivate passengers to be more mindful of the amount of stuff they bring on board. Doesn't this seem ridiculous?

So why not create a frequent flyer program in which passengers are incentivized to minimize the amount of luggage they
bring with them? It could be easy to set up and might work like
this: at check-in, the total weight of checked luggage is already
monitored. So why not assign frequent flyer points based on the
total baggage weight of each passenger? For example, anyone
without checked luggage would get the most bonus points, passengers whose luggage weighed less than 50 lbs (23 kg) would
get the second most, and those with over 50 lbs would receive
none at all. In the same way, the weight or number of carry-on
items could also be monitored and linked to the level of reward
points received. Think about your habits when you travel by plane.
How much superfluous stuff do you take with you? How much of
that could you easily do without if you were motivated to do so?
Do you really need to pack three pairs of shoes for a two-day business trip or bring beach towels to a resort that supplies its own? A
program like the one I'm suggesting would empower passengers

to have control over the number of frequent flyer points they could earn. I may still opt to take unnecessary baggage in situations where that is more important to me than earning points. But when my goal is to earn as many rewards as quickly as possible, I can fast track my progress by minimizing my luggage. It's my choice, and I am in control.

Consider the potential result of such a program. From the airline's perspective, its interests would be immediately aligned with those of its reward-seeking passengers, thereby giving it a strong motivation to promote rather than resent the program. For passengers, such a program would allow a faster accumulation of rewards. But there would be another, supplementary benefit to both. By giving passengers an incentive to pack and travel more efficiently, all the onboard clutter caused by excessive carry-on luggage could be greatly diminished. The result would be a better in-cabin experience for passengers and crew alike as well as more efficient and more punctual flights. Because, let's face it, a key drudgery and time waster on each flight is the stuffing and unstuffing of overhead compartments. Through a program like this, the airlines could boost profitability on multiple fronts (fuel and time savings on each flight) while providing passengers with a more enjoyable in-flight and reward program experience. The name of the program could be changed from frequent flyer to light flyer.

Seems intuitive and appealing, right? So why isn't there an airline already doing it? Could it be that they are so set in their ways, so accepting of operating only within their already established boundaries that they are blind to something so apparent from an unconventional perspective? Airlines are all clamoring to be innovative and customer-centric, so how could they miss something like this? Of course, such a program could eventually be taken to the next level, in which the weight of passengers themselves is monitored, giving them an incentive to be more fit.

That is admittedly more controversial and more encompassing, but it gets much more deeply into the realm of driving lifestyles. Airlines suddenly in the wellness business? Why not? But for now, one step at a time.

As another illustration, have you ever wondered about the outrageous cost of dry cleaning your clothes? You buy a forty-dollar pair of dress pants, and then pay six dollars to dry clean them pretty much after each wearing. In other words, you pay 15 percent of the purchase price of an item just to have it cleaned after a single use.

Using the same ratio, if you own a twenty thousand-dollar car, you would pay three thousand dollars for every car wash! It's absurd. What can possibly be so ridiculously expensive in the relative process of cleaning clothes compared to cleaning anything else? And why do we all accept it as such? There's no pressure from consumers for a fundamental change? Especially given that the experience of going to the dry cleaners is loathed by most consumers, and that dry cleaning is probably not an overly environmentally friendly process in terms of energy use.

The expression "being taken to the cleaners" is clearly no joke. I am sure there have been incremental innovations in the way dry cleaners operate, and of course, stain-resistant or wrinkle-free

fabrics have been introduced that can cut down on the necessary frequency of dry cleaning. But such an out-of-whack cleaning-cost-to-purchase-price ratio seems like a strong justification for more unconventional, radical change. Perhaps the answer is disposable (and recyclable) shirts, suits, and dresses. Anyone with me on this?

Here is a quick test for you. Take a look at the following report from *Fast Company* magazine on the theme of cleaning clothes and ask yourself, to what extent does it reflect the ideas presented so far in this chapter?

> *The "Swirl," a concept washing machine from Germany's Designaffairs Studio, is a soccer ball-like device that cleans clothes during play. Using the device is easy: just stick clothes inside the ball, lock the lid, fill it up with water and let kids play with it to wash and scrub the clothes inside. The device can also double as a water transport system (kick the water in a ball instead of lugging it on your back) and a laundry basket. Designaffairs thinks the ball will somehow enhance the social/cultural relationship between women and children, but hey, it also looks like it could be way more entertaining than going to the laundromat every week.*

Is this story not drenched in unconventional thinking, in reig-niting child play, in turning a mundane chore into a game? It's a disarmingly simple concept, yet with potentially significant impli-cations. Can you resist feeling inspired?

With a couple of examples under our belt of questioning the current limitations of common services, let's turn to products. Let's see how we could rethink an ordinary product to create an exceptional, new consumer experience. You guessed it—I picked a product closely associated with children, but the same mental perspective applies to any industry or offering. The product I have in mind is chocolate. Chocolate is one of the most universally appealing gift items, especially for children. Not surprisingly, locally branded chocolates are prominently displayed as souvenirs at tourist destinations and airports around the world. But what if they could be more than just tasty souvenirs? What if they could also feature educational value and a fun, social game component all in one?

Here's the idea: Imagine a small gift box resembling geo-graphic shapes, such as that of the United States or Europe. Inside the box would be pieces of chocolates, each representing one of the fifty states or one of the countries in Europe (smaller ones can be grouped together to form a single piece), essentially creating a topographical chocolate map. The piece of chocolate corre-sponding to the location where it is purchased, and only that one, would be wrapped and highlighted with a color sticker displaying the name and flag of that state or country, its capital, and popula-tion. For example, a box purchased in San Francisco would high-light the California-shaped piece; a box bought in Dallas would highlight the Texas piece. The rest of the chocolate pieces would remain unwrapped.

Why would such a transformation of souvenir chocolates be meaningful? Because now they can be much more than just sweet treats. They become educational tools that teach

children about geography in a fun, engaging way. And since the bottom of each box would have a map outline onto which children can attach all their acquired stickers, we can create a collection game or contest as well. So if a child has already obtained the chocolate gift box and hence the sticker of several European countries but is missing that of France, he will be motivated to trade with his friends or to request the purchase of a gift box the next time a family member might travel to Paris or Nice. The concept, which I call Chocolate World, elevates a favorite treat to be also an educational tool and a fun collection game, creating multidimensional consumer value. That seems like good business.

Take a step back now. What kind of thoughts and ideas do these examples trigger in your mind? What products and services could you reinvent? How can you use such insights from everyday life or observations from situations where you are the consumer to drive breakthrough concepts for your business?

In August 2006, a fascinating article appeared in *Fortune* magazine entitled "The New Rules." The article targeted the essence of corporate strategy going forward. It provocatively stated that the old strategy that worked well to guide companies at the end of the twentieth century were no longer applicable. The admired principles of Jack Welch (the iconic former chairman and CEO of General Electric whom *Fortune* itself named the Manager of the Century in 1999) needed to be replaced in order to succeed in a drastically changed marketplace. The article proposed a profound turnaround in strategic perspective. It went on to specify a list of new rules to replace the old, including the following:

> **Old Rule:** Big dogs own the street.
>
> **New Rule:** Agile is best; being big can bite you.

> **Old Rule:** Be no. 1 or no. 2 in your market.
>
> **New Rule:** Create something new.

> **Old Rule:** Be lean and mean.
>
> **New Rule:** Look out, not in.

> **Old Rule:** Shareholders rule.
>
> **New Rule:** The customer is king.

What do all these proposed new rules signify to you? Are they not all closely aligned with the perspective of defying conventional wisdom, of aiming to be market driving via sustained consumer relevance and lifestyle enrichment? They sure look that way to me. And while companies back in 2006 may have thought that adopting such new rules was merely optional, after the global crisis of 2008 they can no longer afford to do so. They need to regard it as essential. Just ask GM's former executives.

As an emphatic validation of the *Fortune* article's message, this is what current GE chairman and CEO Jeffrey Immelt said in November 2008: "This economic crisis doesn't represent a cycle. It represents a reset. It's an emotional, social, economic reset. People who understand that will prosper. Those who don't will be left behind."

Speaking of rules, did you consider the origin of all the adopted rules, traditions, and standards that surround your business? In any industry or market there is a strong convergence of how its parameters are defined. There is a general acceptance by competitors around standards for features, pricing, packaging, means of delivery, channels of communication, servicing, and consumer segmentation. For example, why is the in-flight food service among airlines nearly identical yet widely seen as unsatisfactory by consumers? Why are child car seats so similar and complicated that 80 percent of them are installed improperly by parents (according to the National Highway Traffic Safety Administration)?

Who originates these standards? More importantly, why would you ever blindly accept them as given? Let's say that you are the market leader, meaning that you are the one that drives all the standards within your industry or market, the one that all others look to copy. In this case, why would you ever stop continuing to modify and improve the standards, allowing your competitors to catch up to you? Or suppose you are a newcomer into a market space already occupied by sizable, established players. Why would you then accept all the rules by which they already compete, and therefore put yourself at an immediate disadvantage? **Either way, it is to your benefit to continuously challenge the conventional logic of your business environment. You have the golden platform to reconfigure standards in your favor and in**

that of consumers. And once you do this in your business, you can also do it in your personal life.

Let's consider a couple of examples of setting new conventions. The first is about the impact Starbucks had on the café industry by creating its own standards, which then became so persuasive that others simply fell in line and followed. A couple of years ago I was at an independent café and noticed that their coffee size selection and labels had been changed to mirror those of Starbucks: tall, grande, and venti. When I asked the server why, she said: "Pretty much all our customers were asking for their coffee in Starbucks, sizes and lingo, and we got tired of fighting it and decided it was easier just to adopt their standards." If you can't beat 'em, join 'em.

The other example concerns mobile phones and Samsung, the world's leading consumer electronics company from South Korea. Think back to the state of mobile phones in 1998. It's not easy to remember, because the devices have evolved so rapidly, but at that time mobile phones were still primarily focused on providing the best user experience in voice communication. The industry was already quite saturated, dominated by major global players such as Nokia, Motorola, Siemens, and Ericsson. Then along comes Samsung, who not only aspires to crack this industry as a latecomer but sets out to drive the market and become one of its high-end providers. This is nothing short of brazen. Remarkably, Samsung did exactly that. By 2003, just five years later, they had become the second largest global player in mobile phones behind Nokia, had created new industry standards, and had established themselves as a premium brand in the industry. So how did they do it? By daring to challenge industry conventions and using the strategic framework of Value Innovation (the subject of chapter 5). The *Korean Economic Daily* observed:

> *At the time, the talk of the mobile phone indus-*
> *try was which manufacturer can produce the*

smallest-sized handset. Deeply engrossed in the competitive logic, big multinationals all believed that the shortcut to success was to make a mobile phone as small and light as possible. Nonetheless, Samsung broke this conventional thinking with its Value Innovation logic. Samsung noticed that small handsets made it impractical to press buttons, while making the screen smaller as well. Samsung then introduced the "wide & slim" concept for the first time, i.e. make the screens wider and with easy-to-use buttons, and at the same time, make the body slim to increase convenience in carrying it around.

So there you are. In an environment that is impossible to predict, with potential competitors popping up from anywhere and consumers needing to be infatuated, how can you control your own destiny? You need to reclaim your childhood slingshot and kick your ingenuity into high gear. In this sense, your slingshot is not only a symbol of childhood resourcefulness, it's also a symbol of personal empowerment.

"Change the rules before somebody else does."
—Tom Peters, management mastermind
and best-selling author

What are the overall takeaways in terms of strategy and business application?

1 We all had a wide capacity for inventiveness when we were children. By reengaging our childhood creativity, we can recover

the foundation for strategic thinking that defies conventional wisdom and elevates us to the realm of market driving.

2 Unconventional wisdom has been a critical driving force for great accomplishments during the course of human history, and this is well illustrated in the world of sports. Inspiration is all around you; you just need to open your eyes and mind.

3 In a hazardous and unpredictable environment, the role of unconventional thinking is especially critical as a basis of business strategy. When market conditions are unprecedented, traditional ways of operation cannot apply. Instead of a strategy for mere survival that may simply accelerate your company's decline, you should recalibrate your perspective in order to see the environment as full of new, exceptional opportunities.

4 As in your childhood, aim to have a broad inquisitiveness and have this curiosity permeate every facet of your life. Some of the most momentous unconventional ideas for your business will come to you via observations in settings far removed from it.

5 No matter what your market position is, whether you are an established market leader or a newcomer, it is to your strategic advantage to continuously challenge and redefine market standards.

Here's a mental exercise in unconventional thinking. Let your mind wander to the most absurd frontiers of your future strategic options. Then gradually reel them back until they are just within the realm of possible. Kind of like launching your first shot with your slingshot as far as you possibly can, overshooting the target, and then reducing the tension and closing the distance little by little for each subsequent shot until you are able to hit your mark accurately.

The Opossum Test

It's time to take the opossum test. Would you say that your business is like an opossum? Why do I ask? Opossums are seemingly rather ingenious animals. Their principal line of defense against potential predators is feigning death. In other words, the opossum does not accept the conventional wisdom of flight or fight, that in moments of mortal encounters, it has to be either capable of putting up a decent defense or be fast enough to get away. Opossums represent a third alternative. I would also argue that in contrast to other small creatures who devote a large part of their lives to being prepared for predatory attacks—by living in herds, staying very fit, or living in constant fear— opossums figuratively can have a pretty good quality of life. They can go about their business fairly unbothered, and when they sense danger, they just take a nap. Is your business like an opossum, defying accepted norms of conduct and reaping its benefits?

Notice though, that while the opossum's theatrical act is a clever psychological deterrent, it has at least two significant risks if not followed up by subsequent innovations. First, opossums bank on their predators' tastes not changing over time. But what if a stiff, carcasslike appearance suddenly becomes an appetite enhancer and not a suppressant for savage beasts? In this sense, opossums must keep ahead of the changing lifestyle trends of their predators.

Second, the opossum's ploy can only work as long as other animals of similarly low rank on the food chain don't decide to imitate it. Because if every rabbit, squirrel, or deer also started to mysteriously play dead in the path of a cougar or a wolf pack, those predators sooner or later would begin to get suspicious, and the opossum's cover would be fatally blown.

So, is your business like an opossum? Does it have a clearly distinct and unconventional strategy? And are you content with reaping the benefits of some past innovation, or are you continuously re-thinking your business? Let's recall one of the takeaway points from the conclusion of chapter 2: never stop innovating, especially in today's environment of accelerated life cycles, market convergence, and the inundation of consumers with overwhelming choices—all of which puts immense pressure on your offering to retain consumers' attention. Opossums remind us that challenging conventional wisdom and pursuing innovation must both be ongoing processes.

So far I have looked at the insatiable nature of consumers and the strategic goal of being market driving and delivering lifestyle enrichment as a way of staying relevant to consumers and keeping them infatuated. I then proposed that your dormant childhood creativity is your personal reservoir for unconventional thinking, which you can reengage to enable you to be market driving. But once you embrace unconventional thinking, how do you start to turn it into tangible and meaningful insights? In the next chapter I will introduce the use of Accordion Charts, a visual tool that helps to crystallize your thinking.

**"Every child is an artist. The problem is how
to remain an artist once we grow up."**
—Pablo Picasso

The Slingshot Framework

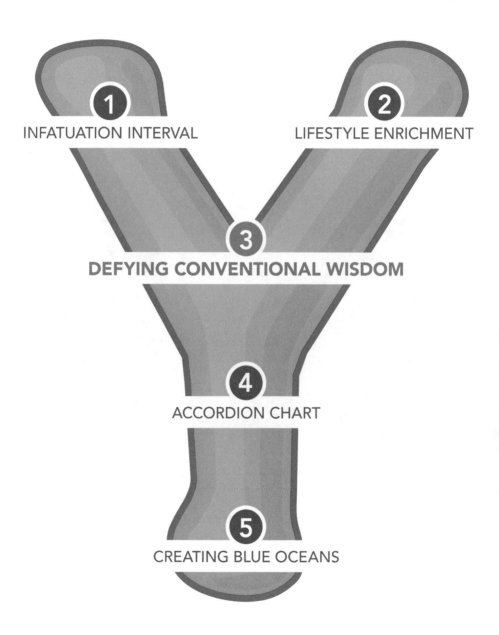

Have you visited **www.slingshotliving.com** lately?
If not, you're missing half the fun and learning.

ACCORDION CHARTS 4

2,400,000 Americans play the accordion
...hopefully not at the same time.
—from inside of a Pepsi cap

In the first century AD, the city of Pompeii in Italy was covered in ash from the massive eruption of nearby Mount Vesuvius. The resulting solidified volcanic debris left behind hollow molds from which casts of victims caught in various poses by the eruption were recreated. They provide fascinating and vivid details of a day gone horribly wrong, as the eruption caught the city's residents completely by surprise. One travel website points out:

> *Since the mountain had last erupted long before anyone alive at the time had been born, people thought that living near the most recognizable landmark looming over the bay of Naples was completely safe. The town had imposing temples, a beautiful forum, perfectly built theater and stadium.*
>
> *It was lunchtime in August 79 AD when Vesuvius began 19 hours of spectacular eruptions. All the people in the 700-year-old town of 20,000 could have escaped. There was time to flee. But no one recognized the inherent danger of the mountain's warnings.*

The body casts of Pompeii are poignant reminders of just how unexpectedly your environment can change and how quickly you can be blindsided by seemingly inescapable dangers. How about you? Will your business be a casualty of rapidly approaching volcanic ash? Or are you continuously scanning your horizons in a way that you won't get caught off guard?

The danger of misjudging trends that can make your business become obsolete is very real indeed. Figuratively, you may have even less time to get out of the way or to decide on a viable action plan than the citizens of Pompeii did. In chapter 3, I touched on the difficult predicament of newspapers in maintaining relevance to consumers, and the more insular focus that Coke had versus that

of Pepsi, which led to the latter making remarkable advances in relative market value. Both of these examples expose the issue of relevance and the need to evolve your offerings so that they have continuous meaning to consumers and are themselves molding lifestyles. Companies can easily run into the trap of defining their business too narrowly, which blocks them from sensing imminent danger, or the trap of obsessing about being the best rather than being the most relevant, which prevents them from seeing significant new opportunities.

Naturally I would like to illustrate this point by evoking some wonderful childhood imagery. Dr. Seuss was a true ambassador of unconventional thinking, and he is the subject of a case study in the final chapter of this book. One of my favorite Dr. Seuss stories is about the Zax, imaginary creatures who can only go in one specific direction and are very stubborn. In the story, two Zax, one southbound, the other headed north, happen to bump into each other in the middle of the desert, each perfectly blocking the other's path. Neither of the two is willing to budge, expecting the other to get out of the way first. And they remain there, nose to nose, obsessed with winning the standoff.

They become so preoccupied with and consumed by each other's presence that they don't notice the world passing them by. Which it does. A new highway is built right around them in the desert. As Dr. Seuss puts it:

> **"And they built it right over those
> two stubborn Zax.
> And left them there, standing
> un-budged in their tracks."**

Similarly, companies that focus too narrowly on beating their competition are in danger of losing out on substantial new market opportunities and of becoming inconsequential to consumers.

Here is a telling business world example of how the mighty can fall when they make this mistake. Until a few years ago, Kodak was sitting on top of the world. Or so it seemed. Founded in 1892, Kodak was an iconic American company whose brand was recognized around the world and synonymous with the market segment it dominated: film photography. Things started quickly to unravel around 2003. Kodak was caught sleeping as the world transitioned from film to digital photography. The company severely misjudged the speed and impact of this transition and its lifestyle implications. Coupled with the rapid convergence around personal portable devices, digital photography empowered consumers to create, edit, store, and share images instantly. As a result, Kodak's core business, in which it was clearly the best, was on a fast track to obsolescence. How could Kodak have miscalculated to such an extent?

And what were the consequences? Well, after seventy-four years, Kodak was delisted from the Dow Jones Industrial 30 Index of leading American companies on April 1, 2004 (which you may note is ironically April Fool's Day). Kodak then embarked on a radical and painful restructuring to reestablish its relevance. It had to cut 25,000 jobs. It posted eight consecutive quarters of losses through the end of 2006, with a single quarterly loss of as much as $1 billion in 2005. Worst of all, the new reality was that even though Kodak quickly became a leader in digital photography, it was not a sustainably profitable business. In simplified terms, the company's core business shifted from being a monopoly to being a commodity in the blink of an eye.

So Kodak had to kick innovation into high gear and look across market segments to find new areas of profitable growth. One area where there seems to be a clear market driving and consumer enrichment opportunity is in battling counterfeiting, which costs American companies an estimated $250 billion annually. According to an article in *Fast Company* in October 2008: "Kodak's new Trace technology uses an odorless, colorless, virtually invisible powder infused into the ink, which can be put into almost any chapter of a product's packaging: paper, plastic, threads, even the adhesive behind a label. And Kodak's proprietary reader is the only device that can read the marker." Kodak is in the process of reinventing itself.

It's interesting to ponder the casualties of irrelevance as we look back on the recent past. In your opinion, what everyday things became irrelevant over the past decade? What can you think of that were in common use just ten years ago but are no longer or barely around today? Here is a list compiled by the Huffington Post in December 2009 of twelve things that became or are on their way to becoming obsolete in the first ten years of the new millennium:

1. Calling

2. Classifieds in newspapers

3. Dial-up Internet

4. Encyclopedias

5. CDs

6. Landline phones

7. Film (and film cameras)

8. Yellow Pages and Address Books

9. Catalogs

10. Fax machines

11. Wires

12. Handwritten letters

Hopefully, you did not find the key offering of your business on the list above. But if you did, what would be far worse is if it caught you by surprise, if this was the very first time you realized the imminent demise of your offering!

"In the future, instead of striving to be right at a high cost, it will be more appropriate to be flexible and plural at a lower cost. If you cannot accurately predict the future then you must flexibly be prepared to deal with various possible futures."
—Edward de Bono, leading creative thinker

In late 2004, shortly before the official release of the Blue Ocean Strategy book, I had a series of meetings with community leaders and prominent business executives in western Michigan. The purpose of the meetings was to herald the exciting premise and methodology of the book, to offer a jump start in applying it to their organizations before the rest of the world, and to explore how its application could help the region as a whole to become a leading hub of innovation. All my meeting partners were receptive, but each asked one critical question: "Who else is already on board locally?" In other words, no one wanted to be first. Here was a business community heavily tied to traditional industries (automotive, furniture, and tool and die). It was a renowned center of manufacturing excellence. Yet regional companies were in danger of becoming irrelevant because of their unwillingness to rethink their businesses in the face of a rapid environmental change. For example, the local tool and die companies' answer to mounting pressure from Chinese competitors was to intensify political lobbying in Washington for restrictive tariffs against imports. So instead of trying to reinvent themselves for continued relevance in a new global economy, they thought they could make the problem go away by putting up walls to artificially keep out unwelcome competition.

Similarly Steelcase, one of the flagship local companies and a global furniture manufacturer, failed to maintain meaningful relevance. This company was a workstyle enrichment pioneer with a long history of innovation, but it became complacent. In 1997, the year when the company went public, the publication *Everybody's Business: A Field Guide to the Leading 400 Companies* said of Steelcase: "This company, more than any other, is responsible for the look of the modern office. Since 1968, they've been the industry leader, earning a reputation as the General Motors of the office furniture industry." So here was a company clearly driving workstyle enrichment. Yet perhaps the comparison to GM was an ominous one, as Steelcase experienced a severe drop of nearly 40 percent in revenues, from $3.8 billion in 2001 to $2.3 billion in 2004, while falling off the Fortune 500 list of the biggest American companies. Its 2009 revenues are back to $3.1 billion, and the company seems to be on a path of revival. But what a humbling lesson in unsustained relevance.

More recently there are promising signs pointing to the resurgence of western Michigan. Grand Rapids, its largest city, is becoming a substantial healthcare hub and has a state-of-the-art convention center that is stimulating hospitality-related activity. In 2009 the city began hosting ArtPrize, an open art competition that gives away the biggest art-related prize in the world. ArtPrize transforms both indoor and outdoor downtown venues to showcase a wide variety of artistic displays over a three-week period, and the organizers defer completely to public opinion to decide which should win the top prize. During the inaugural event, entries by a mix of 1,200 local, national, and international artists attracted over 200,000 visitors, whose votes determined the recipient of the $250,000 first prize. ArtPrize is gaining considerable recognition, with the *Wall Street Journal* labeling it a "model of urban revitalization and public engagement." It is reminiscent of the Cow Parade concept (which I will discuss in a later chapter) and symbolic of the creativity surge that is driving new levels of lifestyle enrichment in western Michigan.

Things on the eastern side of the state are not as rosy. You already know what happened to the Big Three automotive companies of Detroit, having to publicly implore the government for a lifeline in 2008, with GM and Chrysler finally seeking bankruptcy protection and embarking on radical downsizing plans in the spring of

2009. Not surprisingly, the wake of the 2008 economic crisis has left Michigan as one of the hardest hit states in the country, experiencing the single highest unemployment rate among all the states, which in October 2009 stood at 15.1 percent, a full 2 percent higher than that of Nevada, which was second highest at 13 percent, and almost 5 percent higher than the national average of 10.2 percent, according to the Bureau of Labor Statistics. Detroit, the state's largest city, is one of America's fastest dying cities, according to a *Forbes* report in August 2008: "High-unemployment and the continued struggles of General Motors and Ford have left Detroit something of a scrap heap, with stalled growth and a fleeing populace." **Without continuous innovation and a vision to be market driving, an entire region or economy can quickly become irrelevant.**

ArtPrize in Grand Rapids

By the way, the concept of defying conventional wisdom to drive ongoing relevance is not limited to the business world. It has wide-ranging social implications as well. One of the saddest self-imposed limitations of our society is that which is artificially placed around the elderly. Senior citizens are often looked on as obsolete adults and a burden on society's resources. Yet this viewpoint is costly and counterproductive on many levels. It deprives the elderly of proper stimulus, deflates their self-image, and creates a perception of uselessness, which in turn accelerates their depression and physical decline. It is a self-fulfilling prophecy. It also denies society a valuable resource: access to the considerable knowledge that older people have accumulated over their lifetimes. There are immense costs to society of this vicious cycle, as the elderly have been rendered irrelevant by the boundaries placed around them.

How do we break this cycle? I recently read about an example of a very simple solution. The story centered on a school and a nursing home, which are across the street from each other but largely without any contact. The kids at the school were performing poorly because of their inability to read properly. And the residents of the nursing home were quietly living out their lives with less and less meaning. Then the school principal had an idea: why not send the kids across the street after school hours and have the elderly tutor them in reading? This simple idea, which seems so obvious and trivial in hindsight, had not occurred to anyone before because it overstepped the traditional boundaries of conduct and perception. Within weeks, the reading abilities of the kids improved measurably and in a way that did not cost anything. And in the process, the general disposition and quality of life among the nursing home residents was also noticeably elevated because they once again felt relevant. Wow. Better performing, more motivated children. Happier and therefore mentally healthier elderly at no cost. Society wins!

For further musings on the potential societal impact of unconventional thinking, I invite you to read the radical concepts in appendix A. One is about reinventing higher education, while the other, called Lifeline, is about enabling the homeless and the elderly to help each other.

In 2007 I was invited to host an event on corporate strategy in Bogota, Colombia. My featured guest was the former mayor of

Bogota, Enrique Penalosa. He came to talk about the highly successful mass-transit program named Transmilenio that he instituted during his tenure. The system began operation in 2000, after only three years of construction and development, and it accomplished what most locals believed impossible: it transformed one of the most hopelessly congested cities in the world into one with encouraging mobility.

What made this unlikely success possible? Unconventional thinking, of course. Before Transmilenio, Bogota's bus system was absolutely chaotic. It was strung together from thousands of independent and uncoordinated bus operators. There were no specified routes, so drivers could improvise their path. The buses were old and dilapidated, and payment for rides was conducted onboard, causing massive delays. Tinkering with this system would at best lead to incremental improvement in the city's public transportation. What was needed was a new way of tackling the problem, of bypassing the existing framework altogether. Penalosa's initiative was bold and effective. He created fixed bus routes and exclusive bus lanes along the center of avenues (so that passengers walked to and from bus stations on overpaths) for speed, safety, and reliability. The new buses and bus stations were modern and comfortable, which transmitted a positive image, and bus stations handled ticket payments, further expediting the transit experience. Soon after its introduction, Transmilenio was carrying eight hundred thousand people per day, a testament to its  broad relevance. Since then, municipal officials from around the world have come to study and learn from it.

Have I sufficiently convinced you of the need to systematically challenge the conventional boundaries of your business and actively drive its lifestyle enriching relevance? If so, let's now look specifically at how to go about it. When I work with organizations, I don't tell them what to do. Rather, I take on the role of facilitator, provocateur, and objective outsider who leads them to rethink their own strategies. My workshops are based on the premise that no matter how successful, innovative, or unconventional a company already is, its executives still operate within certain assumed barriers of what they can't and shouldn't do. I provoke and challenge participants to overstep these perceived boundaries in order to discover new strategic possibilities and alignment around the best way forward. How do I go about this?

First, I look to establish a general receptivity to unconventional thinking among participants via an exercise that evokes a bit of childlike resourcefulness. Then I move to explore two basic questions:

1 How do you define your business, and how should you define it to unlock greater lifestyle or workstyle enrichment for consumers?

2 Who are your most relevant and not just your most direct competitors?

I find these are pivotal questions for uncovering consequential, new strategic possibilities. By their sheer simplicity, they are quite challenging for executives to answer. So to facilitate the response process, I invite participants to construct a visual snapshot I call an Accordion Chart. **An Accordion Chart is an illustrative tool that enables the flexible exploration of market**

spaces that an organization's offering occupies. It illuminates the full spectrum of the offering's positioning from its core utility to its most general application. It is called an Accordion Chart because, just like the musical instrument, it is collapsible. It can be used to flexibly look across, combine, and integrate various gradations of market detail.

So let's plunge in and get a bit technical. I will define the process for you, and then give an example of its application, followed by a discussion of the important insights generated.

The Accordion Chart Process

- One-page chart showing the current strategic landscape of a company's offering
- The chart allows for visual exploration and understanding of strategic possibilities across market layers
- Process sequence:

1 **Chart Outline:** Create a chart with five to seven vertical columns and labels, as in the example on pages 116–117. Start by filling out the right-most column of the chart by answering the following questions.

2 **Market Definition:** How would you define most narrowly the core utility of your offering to consumers? In other words, what do you provide for them at the most basic level? What specific need or desire do you fulfill?

3 **Competitors:** What competitors also provide the same core utility? Who are your direct competitors in this narrow market segment? List major competitors by name. Others can be clustered.

4 **Market Size and Share:** What is the total size of this market segment, expressed in annual sales volume? What is your market share and that of each major competitor?

5 **Growth Potential:** What is the market segment's growth potential?

6 **Going Up Market:** Now repeat steps 2–5 by going progressively broader in your market definition. Each time, think about what is the one larger market definition of which the previous is a subset, and fill out each column from right to left on the page until you reach the broadest definition possible: your

USING AN ACCORDION CHART

Market Definition

Most Broad Utility      **Most Narrow Utility**

offering's most general utility. As you go broader, you can label competitors in groups and estimate market size and growth rate data that you don't know with certainty. You should aim to have five to seven columns in total.

To show the Accordion Chart in action, I must first challenge you with a trivia question: How far can you stretch a pizza if you put it through an accordion? What on earth can I be talking about? Let me rephrase the question: What if we took an ordinary offering (like preparing and serving pizza) and examined its broadened utility through the Accordion Chart process? What would it tell us? What new insights would we gain about the business?

So here we go with our fictive example of an Accordion Chart application. Suppose you are a regional fast-food pizza chain called Shazam Pizza. You are very good at what you do locally, but you have ambitious plans for expansion. How would you construct your chart? What would it look like? The following step-by-step account relates to the chart below.

First, you want to define your core, central utility to consumers. You decide that the definition that best captures your core essence is "Locally Branded Quick-Service Pizza," which becomes the market segment title of the far right column on the chart. This means that the need and desire you most specifically fulfill is for those consumers who are looking for a quick, locally originated pizza-eating experience. You then identify your key competitors in this segment (Pop, Sparkle, Zing, and others), along with market share labels, total segment size, and growth rate. This column reflects your most immediate competitive environment, and it shows that you are its clear market leader, with a 60 percent share of the region in which you operate.

Next, you want to think about the one-broader market segment definition. In other words, what is "Locally Branded Quick-Service Pizza" most fittingly a subset of in terms of the utility it provides for consumers? In this case, the answer is "Branded Quick-Service Pizza," which then appears as the segment label for the second column from the right. It consists of two main competitor groups: locally branded quick-service pizza restaurants and nationally branded quick-service pizza venues. This one-larger market segment provides fulfillment for those consumers who want a pizza-eating experience but are willing to get it either from a local or a national chain. Notice that the column definition on the right is always a subset of the column to its left. In the second column, the locally branded quick-service pizza's market share is only 30 percent, meaning that while Shazam dominates the narrowest segment in which it operates, that entire segment has only a minority slice of the segment one level up. You again want to label total size and estimated growth rate of this level of market segmentation.

You then go on to the third column from the right the same way, which you tag as "Branded Fast Food." Notice that our column definitions are getting less and less specific, which is precisely the point. It is within this third column that you come face to face with all the affiliated fast-food providers in your region, be it burger, chicken, sandwich, tex mex, etc. Your one-up segment from there is "Informal Eating Out," which includes the various nonbranded sources of quick eating as well. Then you finally arrive at the left-most column, which represents the broadest utility of your pizza restaurants: "Entertainment Destination." This last category includes all the various types of locales where you can be treated to casual food as well as some form of fun or amusement.

Important Takeaway Points About the Use of Accordion Charts

As you systematically continue farther left, notice that your relative size in the marketplace rapidly becomes smaller and smaller and your familiarity with it less and less. You are moving further and further from your comfort zone, from the narrow market segment you are most knowledgeable about. For this reason, aggregated market share, total market segment size, and growth rate figures become more and more difficult to define or even to estimate as you move to the left on the chart. If you are unable to estimate any market data, label it with a question mark, which is your prompt to obtain and fill in additional market information later. **In other words, the Accordion Chart helps to highlight market information that you didn't deem relevant to your business but which in actuality has a bearing on your broader strategic frontiers.** This is part of the eye-opening process, helping to expand your vision.

Another key dimension of your progression from right to left is that at certain points you will find yourself having options as how to label the next up-market segment. For example, when going from branded quick-service pizza in the second column to branded fast food in the third, you opted to continue in the direction of more general definitions of branded food. But you could have just as easily labeled the third column "Pizza Consumption" and proceeded along the dimension of satisfying the more general desire for this specific type of food. Competitors in this segment could have then included Italian casual-dining restaurants, supermarkets (frozen pizzas), and do-it-yourself pizzas. Along this path, the next up-column could be labeled "Italian Food Consumption," under which you would assemble varieties of Italian foods that compete against pizza (spaghetti, lasagna, minestrone, etc). The final, most general column could then be labeled "International Cuisine" and include the key cuisines that compete against Italian (Mexican, French, Chinese, Thai, etc.).

In the chart we constructed, there was an important decision to be made when moving to the left from the "Informal Eating Out" column: should the final one-up segmentation proceed along the dimension of providing primarily a food-related experience, in which case the broadest utility could be labeled "General Eating Out," or should it be something even more encompassing? In this case, the latter was chosen, whose label became "Entertainment Destination." **Anytime you come to such decision points using Accordion Charts, you should proceed to explore each option or at least the most intriguing ones on separate charts, to see where each takes you.** Consequential insights can be generated, not just by looking within a chart, but also by considering the similarities and differences among variations.

What if you are a conglomerate with multiple offerings? In this case, even if they are interrelated, you should construct a separate Accordion Chart for each major offering. This will raise your awareness of their shared and diverging utility. For example, in the case of Apple Inc., you would create Accordion Charts for iTunes, iPod, iPhone, iPad, and iMac separately in order to define each offering's singular core utility and to chart their progression toward the common broader utility on which they all converge.

What if your offering represents a different basic utility to different but large clusters of consumers? This could very well happen. The elderly can perceive the core utility of a mobile phone as an emergency device (safety), while middle-aged adults see it primarily as a business communication tool (staying connected), and teenagers view it as a social platform (companionship, social networking). In this case it makes sense to explore each major consumer group in parallel on separate charts. **Remember, what you are after are new insights on consumer relevance, lifestyle enrichment, and market opportunities, so try all kinds of variations of the Accordion Chart.** Its purpose is to give structure to your exploration.

Lastly, based on my experience of using Accordion Charts with numerous and diverse organizations, the optimal number of segmentation levels you should aim for is five to seven. This range gives enough of a progression to elevate your thinking to sufficiently broad levels of utility without overly diluting it.

Once you have completed your Accordion Chart, what does it tell you? What important insights does it generate? How can these insights be used as a foundation for the unconventional thinking that will allow you to drive markets and lifestyle enrichment?

An Accordion Chart lets you zoom in and out of your offering's utility definition, much like you can zoom in and out when looking at a destination's geographical location on Google Earth. You can see all the market layers you currently compete in as well as all your competitors from most direct to most distant. Therefore you are in a position to examine and answer several key questions:

How Should You Define the Most Basic Utility of Your Offering?

This question forces you to look at yourself squarely from the consumer's perspective in the simplest terms. Companies often tend to overcomplicate and therefore dilute the core essence of what they do. If your core utility can remain relevant to consumers, you can broaden your relevance by building on it instead of replacing it. As an illustration, think back to Nokia. In 1991 it made the decision to abandon its core business of heavy manufacturing as it no longer appeared sustainably relevant. In contrast, since it jump-started the mobile telecom industry, Nokia reached for greater expansion of its offering's utility without diluting its core. Its handheld devices are still mobile communication tools, even

ACCORDION CHART

Most Broad

Market Definition	Entertainment Destination	Informal Eating Out
Competitor Groups (Players)	• IEO • Cinemas • Sports complex & arenas • Malls • Beach /Park • Amusement Parks • Internet Cafes • Book stores • Live music spots • Kids' birthday party destinations	• Branded FF **11%** • Food Courts • Sandwich Shops • Bakeries • Ice Cream Shops • Cafes • Casual Dining • Bars • Gas Stations
Total Market Size	?	$318 billion ?
Growth Potential	?	15% ?

Note: Market size and growth rates are for illustrative purposes only for an unspecified U.S. region, and therefore

EXAMPLE for SHAZAM

Most Narrow →

Branded Fast Food	Branded Quick Service Pizza	Locally-branded Quick Service Pizza
• Branded Pizza **17%** • Branded Burger • Branded Chicken • Branded Sandwich • Branded Mexican • Branded Donut • Branded Coffee • Others	• Local Branded QS Pizza **30%** • Nationally Branded QS Pizza **70%**	• Shazam **60%** • Pop **20%** • Sparkle **5%** • Zing **5%** • Others **10%**
$35 billion	$6 billion	$1.8 billion
4%	1.5%	6%

not necessarily reflective of actual market conditions.

though they are also becoming multifaceted platforms of self-expression, entertainment, networking, and personal business by venturing into such applications as Web browsing, photography, film, television, music, reading, gaming, banking, scheduling, navigation, and security. With Nokia targeting full-on entertainment as the next expansion frontier of its utility, mobile communication may become further refined in the process, but it will still be an anchoring component of the offering.

By Moving Up One Level at a Time, What Is the Most General Utility of Your Offering?

Most executives focus on the dynamics within the most narrow market definition of what they do; therefore, their strategic thinking is limited to the possibilities within those boundaries. When you define the progression and connection from most basic to most general utility, you develop an understanding of overall market relevance to the broadest possible group of consumers. At any point, you find multiple ways or paths for broadening the definition of utility, as illustrated with Shazam Pizza. You can create separate Accordion Charts for each, thereby seeing a burst of market spaces to which you are already connected in some way and which can be the source of future growth and broadened relevance.

Which Segmentation Level Has the Most Growth Potential, and What Are the Implications for Your Business?

In the example of Shazam Pizza, we see a mild 6 percent growth projection within the most narrow market definition in which the company is a market leader. So if Shazam Pizza wants to target growth well above 6 percent (which any ambitious company should), what are its options? The only way to achieve higher growth within the narrowest segment is to take market share away from its direct competitors, which is resource intensive and difficult to maintain. The other possibility is to look outside the segment for additional growth, implying that you have to venture away from the most familiar and most confining boundaries of your business. Which of the higher segmentation levels has the most growth potential for you depends on relative expected growth rates as well as the ease of incorporating their lifestyle-enriching attributes into your offering.

Who Are Your Most Relevant Competitors?

From Shazam Pizza's chart we see that the segmentation level with the most growth potential is the fourth broadest: Informal Eating Out. Although market data is not immediately available for the broadest category of "Entertainment Destination," it is also likely to have promising potential. Based on this observation, Shazam should consider incorporating new elements from these segments and look to players within them as the most relevant competitors for future growth.

Note that on occasion the narrowest segment of your offering can display the highest growth rate on the chart. In this case, the Accordion Chart brings to attention all the broader market levels and up-market competitors who may try to move into your segment, since they see its attractive growth potential relative to theirs. Since some of these may be comparatively large companies with much greater resources, you need to be prepared for their onslaught. The Accordion Chart allows you to understand this in advance and to consider strategies that further differentiate you from such potential infringers.

What Key Variations Can You Think of for Defining Your Offering's Utility, and What New Insights Does Each Definition Generate?

It is important to note that you are not after smaller and smaller fragmentations of your consumers to answer this question, but you are looking for new insights surrounding your perceived utility among major consumer groups. This can lead you to discover new ways of packaging your utility to unlock mass appeal. I mentioned earlier the divergent utility perception of mobile phones by large demographic groups. As another illustration, let's look at McDonald's in the early 1990s, when the company had the opportunity to foray into Eastern Europe for the first time. What if we looked at this prospective market opportunity by constructing two Accordion Charts, one for the restaurant chain's perceived utility by U.S. consumers, and the other by new consumers in eastern Europe? What insights would we gain by such a comparison?

For U.S. consumers, McDonald's represents fundamentally a quick-service food destination. Consumers in eastern Europe viewed McDonald's differently. They have just shed the long and oppressive era of Communism and gained previously unimaginable access to Western offerings. For them the chart would reveal an additional, perhaps even more powerful and fundamental utility dimension: freedom of choice and access to things previously forbidden (the powerful psychological draw I touched on in chapter 1). For the mass of new consumers all across eastern Europe, going to McDonald's was as much about celebrating as it was about eating. No wonder that the first McDonald's restaurant in Moscow was the single busiest in the world after its opening in 1990. By highlighting such a divergence in basic utility across major consumer groups, Accordion Charts help to pinpoint ways you can be most relevant to each.

What Seemingly Unrelated Dimensions Should You Incorporate Into Your Offering?

This is one of the most eye-opening revelations of Accordion Charts. By seeing on a single page the utility levers and competitors from narrowest to broadest definitions, you can flexibly think about incorporating elements from any of them into your offering in order to drive its future relevance. When you do this, you are jumping across traditional market boundaries and starting to think as a true market driver. Remember, the sources of some of the most powerful innovations are other, seemingly distant businesses whose key success elements you can repackage and incorporate into your own offering. Think here about Cirque du Soleil, which was founded in 1984 by a band of Canadian street performers. The company created an entirely new form of live entertainment by blending elements from several previously separate platforms: circus, theater, opera, and ballet. The resulting spectacle was much more enriching and therefore relevant to a mass of consumers. While only a relatively small consumer pool attended the traditional circus, its newfound combination with

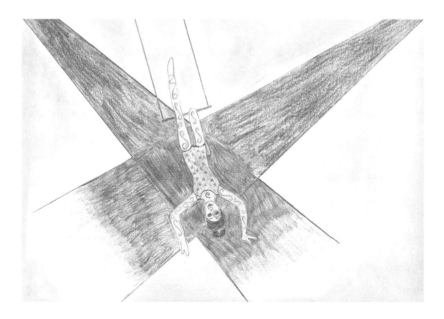

elements of theater, opera, and ballet became attractive to waves of consumers around the world who gladly paid a hefty premium compared to the price of traditional circus to attend. Cirque du Soleil has performed in front of nearly one hundred million spectators worldwide, rolled out nineteen different shows in 2009, and has become one of the most recognized global brands. This is the power of combining traditionally separate dimensions across market segments.

How Can You Move from Right to Left on the Chart?

Ah, yes, I saved the best for last. I think this is the most important question the Accordion Chart draws your attention to. No matter which level of market segmentation exhibits the highest growth potential on the chart, there is always a benefit in expanding the relevance of your offering to its broadest possible definition. This simply has to do with the sheer number of potential consumers you become relevant to as you move from right to left on the chart. Look at the Shazam Pizza example again. In the narrowest definition, the total market size is $1.8 billion. By the time we ascend to "Informal Eating Out" toward the left, that number becomes $318 billion, and we can speculate that the market size of "Entertainment Destination" would be additional multiples of that.

So if you are a player only in the most narrow market segment, you are only relevant to people who are looking to satisfy a need or desire for locally branded quick-service pizza. These are people who have already made the decision that they want to eat, that they want to eat quickly, that they want to eat pizza, and that they want to eat a locally originated pizza. In other words, you don't pop into their minds as a potential solution to their need or desire until it is already very clearly defined. In contrast, if your offering could register in people's minds as a possible solution at the point when only a general craving is conceptualized, then suddenly you could appear relevant to

a mass of consumers. In the Shazam example, the Accordion Chart reveals that this point could be elevated to precede even the need or desire to eat by making consumers perceive your pizza restaurant as an attractive entertainment destination, a place to have fun and eat something good.

To fully grasp the last point, it may help to consider a reverse perspective of the Accordion Chart for a moment. Think of a consumer with a very general need or desire (in Shazam's example, the general desire to be entertained and to eat) who is standing in an empty room with numerous doors. Each door represents a potential solution to the consumer's general craving. Once he chooses a door, he then finds himself in a smaller room, which represents a more specific definition of his need or desire. Doors from this room symbolize further, more specialized solutions, and the consumer proceeds through numerous iterations until the final room has only doors that represent a single, final solution. In Shazam's case, the final doors would all represent locally branded quick-service pizza restaurants, and one among them would be Shazam. But if your offering is behind one of the final doors, think about

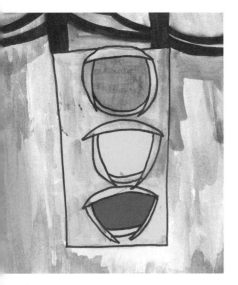

how many rooms a consumer would have to navigate through to get to you and how small the chance that your door will be the one selected from among all those along the way. In contrast, if your offering could be behind one of the first doors and be so infatuating and fulfilling that the consumer needs to go no farther (if Shazam could be perceived as an attractive entertainment destination *and* a provider of good food), it would have commanding lifestyle relevance to a wide band of consumers.

"Let there be a light!"   Accordion Charts motivate you to broaden the relevance of your offering to a significantly wider audience and also draw your attention to where such opportunities reside. How to turn these insights into specific strategies can be best addressed via the process of Blue Ocean Strategy, which is the topic of the next chapter.

Staying with the fast-food theme for a bit longer, a few years back I had the pleasure of taking a stroll in downtown Chicago with Mike Roberts, then president and COO of McDonald's. We were talking about innovation, and as we passed near a McDonald's restaurant, I mentioned an off-the-cuff idea of how the concept of fast food, and of drive-through in particular, could be looked at in a slightly new dimension, and how such a small tweak in perspective could potentially unlock significant consumer value and differentiation. First, let's think about the core utility of a drive-through: it's about eating on the run. So the offering needs to be fast and convenient. Yet how do drive-throughs typically work today? They wind around the entire restaurant building. As an approaching consumer, you have no way of clearly seeing the number of cars ahead of you in the queue. Only after you already commit yourself by ordering and proceeding around the corner of the building do you see the total number of cars before you. This means that you have no way to accurately judge the amount of time it will take to pick up your order and go. This is a problem especially during peak meal hours. And if speed is the most important priority for you, you will find this experience frustrating.

Here is a possible solution: what if there was a way to indicate to speed-conscious consumers the approximate waiting time before they get in line? For example, what if the restaurant had a traffic light indicator that approaching consumers could see from a distance which would signal the current drive-through waiting time? A green light could mean virtually no waiting, a yellow light a less-than-five-minute wait, and a red light a wait of over five minutes. This kind of early alert system, which does not seem overly investment-intensive, would create a lifestyle enrichment differentiator for consumers. Additionally, it would motivate restaurant employees to be more efficient by striving to maintain at least a yellow level throughout the day, as managers could now continuously monitor the speed of their service.

How might we arrive at such an idea using Accordion Charts? As we proceed to define our offering's utility in broader and broader terms, what if we chose speed as the key utitlity driver? So instead of showing more general segmentations of providing a food venue on the chart, we explored segmentations of providing speed. This seems quite relevant especially for the drive-through component of fast-food restaurants. In this case, we might define our market segment categories moving from most specific to most general as "Drive-Through Restaurants," "Speed of Eating," "Speed of Necessary Daily Activities," "Speed of

Necessary Activities," and "General Speed of Living." Such a chart would display entirely new market arenas and competitors, all of which share the commonality of injecting speed into the busy life of consumers.

Viewing the chart would then lead us to think of ways to break down conventional barriers to the speed of the drive-through experience and to borrow concepts from faraway businesses that converge on the chart that have successfully enhanced speed for their consumers. As such, under the wider market segmentation of "Speed of Necessary Activities," we could include barbershops and hair salons as a competitor group, leading us to discover the success of the QB House, Japan's largest chain of barbershops. Founded in 1996, the QB House succeeded in challenging the deep traditions of Japanese hair-cutting ritual, which was time consuming and expensive. In contrast, it defied conventional wisdom and focused purely on the speed and low price of delivering a basic men's haircut. In a 2003 *Wall Street Journal* article, Kuniyoshi Konishi, the founder of QB House, explained: "Newcomers can topple the status quo by appealing to Japanese consumers' overwhelming hunger for more choices and greater innovation. Imagine yourself as the end user and then look for how the end user is inconvenienced. Look for areas of dissatisfaction, and here you will find your business opportunity."

One of the key elements to QB House's innovation was (you guessed it) the installation of light indicators in front of each barbershop. A green light signified no waiting inside, a yellow light a five-minute wait, and a red light up to fifteen minutes. So here lies a wonderful shortcut, a veritable wormhole to success. **Once you generate insights on how to advance your offering's relevance, you don't have to invent its delivery platform. You can mimic or emulate the success examples of remote businesses.** But somehow you have to be able to identify those remote businesses and success examples which are applicable to your business. This is the path of exploration that Accordion Charts leads you down.

> **"Because ideas have to be original only with regard to their adaptation to the problem at hand, I am always extremely interested in how others have used them."**
> —Thomas Edison, American inventor (1847–1931)

Most senior executives will tell you that innovation is one of the key strategic drivers of their organizations. If this is the case, then one variation of the Accordion Chart you should construct is the positioning of your company along the dimension of being an innovator—from its most narrow to its most broad definition as it relates to your business. This has two tangible advantages. First, it makes you think about the relevance of innovation in its own right to consumers, distinguishing between self-serving and meaningful innovation. Second, it expands your vision to consider trailblazing innovators regardless of industry or geographic location as your competition, motivating you to excel further. If innovation really is an important differentiator, then wouldn't you want to be recognized across markets as one of the best at innovation?

Let's again revert to McDonald's. In 2006, the company barely made the top one hundred list of the world's most innovative companies as compiled by *BusinessWeek* and Boston Consulting Group. It was the very last company on the list, at the one hundredth position. Here is an organization that feeds over fifty million people a day around the world, a clear market leader with a globally recognized brand, and with an offering that appears to have continuous relevance to consumers. Yet McDonald's is not satisfied with simply maintaining its position. So alongside the pursuit of operational excellence, it continues to explore ways to create even deeper relevance for consumers. This means innovation. Over the past few years McDonald's has actively revamped its restaurants into entertainment destinations, putting an increased emphasis on maintaining consumers' attention not just during meal times but in between meals as well.

Their initiatives include the McCafé (a premium coffee shop venue and range of associated offerings within the restaurants), Wi-Fi zones, flat-screen televisions, and reconfigured, more comfortable interiors. At the start of 2010, McDonald's did away with user fees and offered limitless, free Wi-Fi to consumers. "We're not just about hamburgers," said Dave Grooms, chief information officer for McDonald's. "We are about convenience and all kinds of value. We don't mind at all if people take advantage of the Wi-Fi and linger a bit." Wow! McDonald's actually wants consumers to linger in their restaurants, and not just to come and go quickly to consume burgers. This is the type of insight that Accordion Charts help to generate when you are open to re-imagining your business. On the 2009 global list of Top Innovators, McDonald's has already moved up to number nineteen. **Clearly the pursuit of meaningful innovation is not a substitute for operational excellence. The two need to be and can be targeted simultaneously.** McDonald's is doing both by continuously perfecting its mealtime offerings while also expanding its relevance as an entertainment destination.

We should also revisit Coke and Pepsi for a moment. I mentioned previously about the shifting relevance of carbonated soft drinks in an increasingly health-conscious society. As a maker of carbonated beverages, how should you define your progression toward more general utility? Who are your most relevant competitors? These are, of course, questions for an Accordion Chart. Most probably you would identify "American-Branded Carbonated Soft Drink" as your core utility, and then progress along increasingly wider definitions of beverages until you reach the general utility of "Thirst Quencher." Along the way you would pit yourself against competing soft drinks, juices, vitamin drinks, dairy, bottled water, etc. This may give you some interesting insight in itself, but the problem is that along the dimension of "Thirst Quencher," your offering is increasingly on the defensive. It is perceived as an unhealthy alternative.

What if, instead, you could go on the offensive and shift the definition of the wider utility of your offering? What if rather than a thirst quencher, you defined it as a "Moment of Indulgence," as a daily treat to yourself? In this case you could get away from having to continuously defend and justify its detrimental health effects and focus on its pure enjoyment value. You are shifting growing consumer guilt back to a basic pleasure. When you construct an Accordion Chart along this dimension, you break out of the more traditional perspective of your overall utility and find yourself sharing market space with other indulgence providers, be it an ice cream, a bubble bath, a trashy novel, a lottery ticket, or even (dare I say it?) a cigarette. Such exploration leads you to elevate your thinking to new frontiers of strategic possibilities.

What are the overall takeaways in terms of strategy and business application?

1 From the perspective of relevance, you need to keep your finger on the pulse of your offering without pause. Without it, your offering can rapidly become inconsequential to consumers.

2 The Accordion Chart is a visual tool that allows you to define and expand the relevance of your offering by exploring the following questions:

- How should you define your offering's most basic utility?
- By going up one level at a time, what is the most general utility of your offering?
- Which segmentation level from most narrow to most broad has the most growth potential?
- Who are your most relevant competitors?
- What major variations can you think of in defining your offering's utility?
- What seemingly unrelated dimensions should you incorporate into your offering?
- How can you shift the positioning of your offering from its most basic utility to its most general?

3 Accordion Charts serve as the platform for the application of unconventional thinking to your business. Specifically, they generate insights on how to drive relevance in the pursuit of infatuation and lifestyle enrichment for the broadest band of consumers possible.

 **USING AN ACCORDION CHART**

Market Definition

Most Broad Utility  **Most Narrow Utility**

4 No matter how market driving your business may already be, you still operate within certain assumptions and mental boundaries. Accordion Charts help you to see where these limitations lie and how to overstep them. So let your imagination and ingenuity lose by playing the accordion!

Now that we have laid the foundation for creative thinking and are asking the right questions, we need a system for turning the resulting insights into tangible strategies. In the next chapter, I will explore the application of Blue Ocean Strategy for this very purpose.

The Slingshot Framework

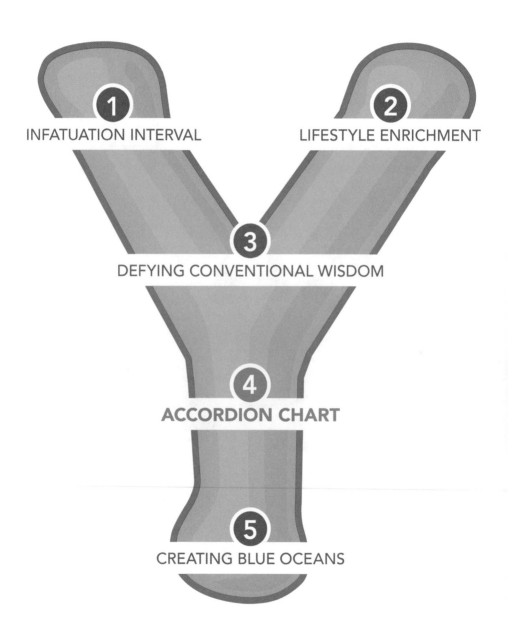

INFATUATION INTERVAL

LIFESTYLE ENRICHMENT

DEFYING CONVENTIONAL WISDOM

ACCORDION CHART

CREATING BLUE OCEANS

Have you visited **www.slingshotliving.com** lately?
If not, you're missing half the fun and learning.

CREATING 5
BLUE OCEANS

You cannot discover new oceans unless you have the
courage to step away from the shore.
—André Gide, 1947 Nobel Prize–winning author

*There once lived a well-known shepherd who would
go to the top of high mountains to buy sheep from
the mountain dwellers. Then he would bring his
new flock down to the valley and sell the sheep for
a hefty profit at the village market. He would often
pontificate that the secret of his success was to buy
"high," sell "low."*

In stark contrast to the wisdom of this parable, the perspective
and methodology of Blue Ocean Strategy have universal appli-
cability. The concept, conceived by Professors W. Chan Kim and
Renée Mauborgne, is the subject of numerous influential articles
and the 2005 international best-selling book of the same name.
Organizations of all sizes, from start-ups to multinationals, and
in any market or industry can benefit from its alluring logic and

**Your New
Mantra for
Success:**
Buy High,
Sell Low

liberating process of simplification, which explains why the book has sold over two million copies and has been translated into more than forty languages (among them Icelandic and Mongolian).

I had the good fortune to be a student of Professor Kim back in 1989 when I did my MBA studies at INSEAD in Fontainebleau, France. Among the great faculty collected there, he clearly stood out and was my favorite professor. I found his views on strategy fresh and compelling and his abundant energy contagious. We became friends and kept in touch after my graduation. Consequently in 1999, after Professors Kim and Mauborgne completed the research that became the backbone of Blue Ocean Strategy, I was among the first to get involved in propagating the concept and enabling organizations to understand and apply its power. In the years since, I have worked with dozens of companies around the world to help them create distinctive strategies based on Blue Ocean Strategy and have used it as the basis for my own business initiatives.

In a nutshell, **Blue Ocean Strategy is a systematic approach for transforming unconventional ideas into successful strategies.** Its core premise is the simultaneous pursuit of differentiation and lower cost in such a way that new demand is created. Although Blue Ocean Strategy sets forth a complete management blueprint from strategy formation to rapid implementation, change management, and organizational leadership, my focus here is on its starting platform of successful strategy formation. That is the point of connection to the sequence of ideas in this book.

> **"Every organization will have to learn to innovate —and innovation can now be organized and must be organized—as a systematic process."**
> —Peter Drucker (1909–2005), writer,
> business consultant, father of modern management

With all the pieces laid out in the previous chapters, let's revisit the progression of concepts in the Slingshot Framework.

The Slingshot Framework

Consumers by nature are insatiable; therefore you need to keep them continuously or extendedly infatuated.

In order to infatuate, your offering must reflect compelling life-style (or workstyle) enrichment and stay relevant to consumers.

Ongoing lifestyle enrichment is achieved by daring to be market driving and to defy conventional wisdom. Reconnecting with your childhood creativity and sense of limitless exploration is your personal reservoir for this thinking process.

The Accordion Chart is a visual tool that enables you to channel unconventional thinking into strategic insights.

Such insights can be systematically shaped into successful strategies through the application of Blue Ocean Strategy.

The Slingshot Framework

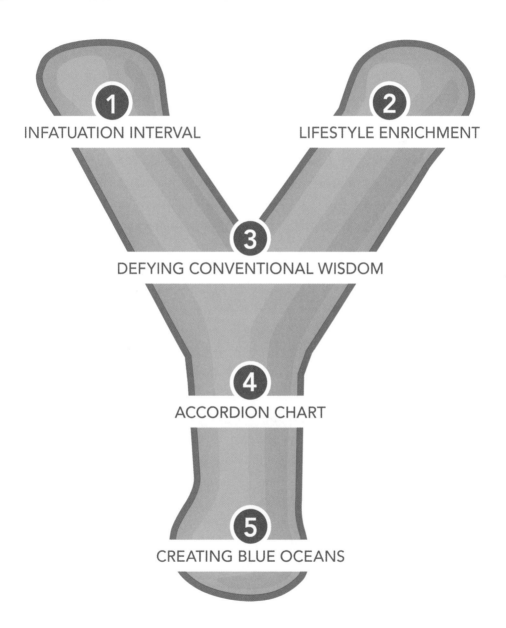

Have you visited **www.slingshotliving.com** lately?
If not, you're missing half the fun and learning.

We find ourselves at the final stage of the framework, at the base of the slingshot on the chart above. So now we can home in on the provocative cornerstone of Blue Ocean Strategy that defines the exact formula for strategic success. It is labeled **Value Innovation** and states that, in successful strategies, differentiation and lower cost are pursued simultaneously in a way that new demand is created, which leads to uncontested (or Blue Ocean) market space. Notice that this in itself is a seemingly counterintuitive concept, going against traditional management views that profess you can do one or the other, be either a highly differentiated or a low cost provider, but not both.

So how does it work? Revisiting Cirque du Soleil gives us a good indication. Cirque du Soleil is credited with resuscitating the circus industry, which was becoming a dying dinosaur of live entertainment. Children are less and less interested in going to the circus compared to previous generations, because there are so many other diversions competing for their attention. So Cirque du Soleil did not try to revive the traditional circus formula, which would have been futile. Instead it rearranged its components to make itself relevant. It eliminated those elements that were costly and no longer appealed to the audience (such as animal acts, star performers, and multiple show surfaces) and replaced them with compelling elements borrowed from other types of live performances (such as a theme, story line, original music, dance, and rich pageantry). It is this type of reallocation of focus and resources from the traditional circus genre that oversteps conventional boundaries to create simultaneous differentiation and lower cost. If you do this in a way that enriches consumer lifestyles, then you can attract a mass following and create your own

Blue Ocean market space—even at a price point much higher than that of traditional circus. Cirque du Soleil did just that, as we noted in the previous chapter.

Inspired by Cirque du Soleil, what examples can you think of where a company has eliminated some dimension or element from its offering, and consumers viewed it as more enriching? Can you think of any such experiences where you were the consumer? Give this a bit of time and see what you come up with, because if you dig deep enough you will discover that so many examples are all around you.

Here are a couple of my personal favorites. In 1985, while studying at the University of St. Andrews in Scotland, I attended a classical guitar concert in town. When I entered the building, I was greeted with something unexpected. The stage and chairs from the concert hall had been removed and the room stood empty. At the entrance was a huge pile of diverse pillows and a sign that invited spectators to take off their shoes, grab as many pillows as they wanted, and proceed into the hall to freely configure their own sitting environment anywhere on the floor. In lieu of a stage, the guitarist's performance stool was in the center of the room, so people could surround him on all sides. I chose five or six cushy pillows and arranged a very comfortable, supine position for myself near the performer. As I looked around, everyone else was in a similarly individualized, relaxed formation throughout the hall.

The so-called Pillow Concert was incredibly enriching. It allowed me to be completely absorbed in the music and to enjoy a live performance on my own terms. Think about what happened here from a strategic perspective. Ordinarily, a couple of the key elements of a live performance venue are the quality of staging and the comfort level of audience seats. These to a large extent determine the experience of spectators and performers alike. But what happened in this concert? Instead of competing on, or being judged on, relative stage decor and seating comfort vis-à-vis other venues, the Pillow Concert eliminated both elements completely. In their place, something new, unconventional, and disarmingly unsophisticated was substituted: a heap of pillows. By doing so, the maintenance and operational cost, as well as the technical requirements of the concert hall, were substantially reduced, and simultaneously, differentiation for the consumer was achieved. In fact, both spectators and performer received a more enriching, closer bonding experience. Note also the transition here, which I spoke about previously in reference to Chris Bangle's comment that "every consumer is a designer" and that forward-looking companies should strive not to create a perfect design to wow consumers but rather to enable consumers to create the perfect design for themselves. An obscure Pillow Concert in a Scottish town was already doing this back in 1985.

I found a more recent and even simpler example: air travel. Whenever you embark on a long trip with multiple layovers, you would traditionally receive multiple boarding passes—one for each flight segment. A layer of difficulty and hassle arises from having to keep these boarding cards in order, remembering which one you can discard and which one you still need as your trip progresses. I have always found this annoying. Therefore, I gleefully noticed awhile back that Northwest Airlines (which has since been acquired by Delta) started issuing a single boarding pass that listed all the connecting flights of an itinerary. Again, what a simple yet double-barrel idea: it simultaneously cuts cost and boosts environmental friendliness for the airline (in having to use less paper, less ink, and less energy) and improves consumer experience via the elimination of superfluous travel documents. I am waiting to see if Delta, once Northwest is fully absorbed, will keep this simplified boarding pass system going.

Both of these examples are seemingly trivial, but that is precisely the point. **Blue Ocean moves can be done at all levels of an organization and with any dimension of an offering. Often the most powerful ones seem insignificant and simple in hindsight, but they unlock considerable consumer enrichment.**

Think about how apparently trite both of my examples appear on the surface. But their effect is profound. The Pillow Concert still sticks in my memory some twenty-five years later as one of my all-time favorite cultural experiences, because the chairs and performance stage were removed. Similarly, the single boarding pass for me is a differentiator. Other things being equal, I would choose Northwest over another airline for this extra convenience, all because some excessive documentation was removed.

In the late spring of 2010, I took my family on a holiday adventure across Europe. We rented a minibus and drove between the Languedoc wine region of France and Budapest, Hungary. Along the way we had the chance to experience the highway toll systems of different countries and note the stark differences among them. Here is the funny thing: the farther east we drove, the more efficient and user-friendly they became. In France, which has a long-established highway system, there is a large network of tollbooths for extracting payment from motorists. The seemingly random intervals and fees add to the aggravation of frequent stops, queues, and delays that drivers face. At the same time, such toll stations are expensive to build and to operate and not so pretty to look at. At some stations I counted fifteen booths in each direction.

Italy was next. In Italy, things worked much more smoothly. We received a ticket at a tollbooth upon entering the country, and we didn't have to make another stop until we were near the border on the other side. At that point we presented the ticket and paid a fee based on the total distance traveled. Then came Slovenia, a small, mountainous country that was formerly part of Yugoslavia and whose highways have been freshly built. Here, the highway fee collection system sidesteps the use of tollbooths altogether. Instead, drivers purchase a sticker at a gas station corresponding to the length of time they intend to use the country's highways (ranging from one week to one year) and apply them to the windshield of their car. Drivers are then free to use any of the country's highways. The only pitfall is the bother of having to attach and remove the stickers.

Last on the journey was Hungary, which has an even more liberating approach. As with Slovenia, Hungary's highway infrastructure was built over the last twenty years, after it emerged from decades of Communism. It was therefore able to leapfrog the traditional payment system still prevalent in western Europe in favor of a solution that makes good use of new technologies. Motorists can buy a pass to use all the national highways simply by sending a text message on their cell phone to a designated number, indicating their car's license plate number and the desired duration of use (from a few days to a year). The charge is added automatically to the driver's monthly phone bill. They can do this at any time and anywhere, prior to using the highways. In effect, the payment process is completely removed from the driving experience itself. To ensure complicity, mobile control stations are set up to scan license plates on the highways and match them against a central database of authorized vehicles.

As with the previous two examples, my highway tale is a tangible showcase of Value Innovation principles in action. Compared to France, the system in Hungary significantly increases consumer value—making highway travel safer and more efficient and comfortable by removing frequent, required stops—because the flow of traffic is not artificially interrupted. At the same time, it also greatly lowers costs—as a software application handling payment and a few mobile control stations replace the considerable infrastructure investment and operating expense of tollbooths. Lastly, the system opens up new demand—motorists are likely to use the roads more because of the simplicity of payment, so they can travel more efficiently, more predictably, and with fewer hassles.

But there is an additional dimension to the story. It shows how the smart application of emerging technologies can be harnessed to drive lifestyle enrichment, in this case providing a much more comfortable, efficient, and safe driving experience. Such meaningful uses of technology can also allow companies to quickly bypass more established competitors who are heavily invested in providing traditional offerings of lesser consumer value. Likewise, a recently democratized country like Hungary can spring ahead of a leading industrialized one like France in the operation of its highway infrastructure.

What happens when you are unable or unwilling to create Blue Oceans? The antithesis of Blue Ocean market spaces are Red Oceans. Red Ocean environments represent the existing boundaries of conventional wisdom. Their familiarity provides a false sense of comfort to companies, because Red Oceans are crowded, confining, and make companies focus on outdueling one another rather than delivering lifestyle enrichment to consumers. The resulting strategic emphasis is insular and resource intensive, limits growth, and runs the real danger of rendering companies or entire industries irrelevant.

A common occurrence within Red Ocean environments is the convergence of competition strictly around price, otherwise known as commoditization. When this happens, all companies simply try to provide the cheapest offering, and consumers have no emotional connection, no infatuation with any particular one. As soon as a lower priced offering becomes available, they switch to it. So unless a company is sure to be the lowest priced provider, it can quickly cease to be relevant. Here is a perfect illustration that every last penny counts in Red Oceans.

In January 2009, Reuters reported:

> In a southern England town, families hit by the financial crisis put a pound store out of business by flocking to a 99 pence shop that opened across the road. The Pound World in Poole saw its earnings plummet by 70 percent and was forced to close within weeks of 99p Stores launching on the other side of the High Street. "It's funny to think a shop can close down because of a penny difference, I suppose it's a sign of the times," customer David Fitzpatrick told The Star newspaper.

Consider for a moment the pervasive Red Ocean mentality that has materialized in the realm of men's razors—a situation so transparently absurd that it has become the butt of satirical comedy. Here is the short of it: leading razor manufacturers such as

Gillette and Schick (who together dominate 80 percent of the U.S. market for razors and blades) attempt to outduel each other by periodically introducing "new and improved" razors. Each new series is touted to offer a much improved shaving experience, but in reality what consumers see is the continuous, incremental increase in the number of blades and the accompanying higher price point. This is leading to a mounting consumer backlash and jettisoning in favor of disposable razors, as well as some humorous chiding. The *Wall Street Journal* reported:

> New razors have been fodder for parody for more than a quarter century. In 1975, the inaugural episode of "Saturday Night Live" included a mock commercial for a three-blade razor with the slogan, "Because you'll believe anything."
>
> The introduction of Gillette's Fusion razor, kept secret until its debut in 2005, was eerily predicted the year before by the satirical Onion newspaper, which ran a fake memo from a shaving executive bragging about besting a competitor's four-blade razor by making one with five.

But if you find yourself in a cutthroat marketplace (no pun intended), take heart in the example of the single boarding pass from earlier. The single boarding pass's apparent triviality has invigorating strategic implications. Namely, how little it can take for your consumer to notice and appreciate a differentiated offering. Given an environment with a high level of similarity among competitors—as with the airlines—you can find nuggets of seemingly negligible differentiators that will generate a disproportionately large and positive consumer response. You just have to have the strategic desire and framework to seek them out.

A lingering and dangerous misconception in Red Oceans is that being big means being resilient. This is a point I touched on earlier in relation to GM. Being resilient is about flexibility, not sheer size. If anything, large size in itself can be a burden. Here is a historical illustration of the spectacular and tragic consequences of getting this wrong. Naturally it has an aquatic theme—consistent with our current oceanic imagery.

The *Vasa* was built to be the mightiest, most fearsome warship of its time. It was constructed in the 1620s under the orders of Sweden's ambitious king, Gustavus Adolphus. At the time, Sweden was at war with Poland, and having a dominant navy was critical to the king's plans to forge an empire around the Baltic Sea.

The ship had unprecedented proportions. With sixty-four guns on two levels and three hundred soldiers on board, it would easily overpower any enemy vessel. The *Vasa* set sail on August 10, 1628, from Stockholm in front of a crowd of awestruck spectators and foreign dignitaries. It fired a salute and proceeded out of the harbor. But it never made it out. Due to faulty design, the ship tipped to one side and sank before its maiden voyage, before tangling with a single foe, just a few hundred meters from shore. It was brought to the surface in 1961 nearly intact and now serves as an intriguing historical museum. According to the museum's brochure, "the ship is so large that you can't photograph the whole thing at once."

The tragic fate of the *Vasa* is a foreshadowing for any company mistakenly counting on its sheer size to stay buoyant, to stay successful. **In the same way that the *Vasa* was not seaworthy, not fit to sail the oceans, an organization lacking adaptability will not be marketworthy, not fit to thrive in today's capricious environment.**

An organization that is finding itself in a very *Vasa*-like predicament is the U.S. Postal Service. Why? The post office is a massive, 235-year-old organization (Benjamin Franklin was appointed the first postmaster general in 1775) with over 600,000 employees (making it the second largest civilian employer in the United States behind Walmart), 250,000 vehicles (the largest civilian car fleet in the world), and 32,000 post offices nationwide. Yet its core business is rapidly becoming irrelevant. With the advent of e-mail and text messaging, people are sending physical letters less and less. The decline is precipitous, with the number of first-class letters delivered by the postal service down 13 percent in 2009 from the year prior. As things stand, the post office is predicting colossal losses of $238 billion over the next ten years, and no incremental tampering with its operations is going to fix that. Rather, the post office needs to reinvent itself altogether in order to stay relevant to new lifestyles, as its competitors (FedEx and UPS) are doing. But given its gigantic size, such change will be a monumental challenge indeed.

If you want further food for thought, consider this statistic: In 1958, the average length of time a company remained on the S&P 500—the index of the most significant, publicly traded U.S. companies—was fifty-seven years. By 1983, it had dropped to thirty years. In 2008, it was just eighteen years. The reign of companies on the biggest list is getting shorter and shorter, as size alone is no longer the key component to keeping them there.

> **"The entire global economy today
> requires Blue Ocean Strategy."**
> —Bruce Nussbaum, innovation editor,
> BusinessWeek

One thing that is clear in the wake of the 2008 global economic crisis is that traditional ways of doing business no longer hold. Trying to do what you did before better or more intensely can no longer be the basis of any sound strategy. By definition, we are living in an unprecedented business environment, and therefore your strategy also must go beyond conventional thinking. But we can also look at our turbulent surroundings in a different way. We can see them as one big Blue Ocean of unexplored market spaces, full of opportunities for the taking. But you may be skeptical. You may wonder how we can be talking about great opportunities when you are fighting for your survival.

It's important to recall the downhill skiing scenario from earlier. The point of the story was that leaning back when descending an uncomfortably steep hill in the hope of maintaining control is much like companies slashing costs during tough times in hope of survival. The effect of both is to exaggerate the danger. **So here is the critical distinction: searching for Blue Oceans implies looking to cut costs—it is a core component of Value Innovation. But this cost cutting is not done blindly. Instead, it is done by reallocating resources from those that are expendable to those that fuel the continued growth of your company.** That is why you need to embrace it. But how? How should you take advantage of this mental recalibration in order to sharpen your perception of Blue Ocean opportunities?

The musings that follow are to assist you in grasping the Blue Ocean Strategy mind-set. First, imagine that you are a world-class athlete, and you have your sights on winning a gold medal at the next Olympics. What key factors of competition would you most need to possess in order to realize your goal? Most likely you would answer that access to world-class facilities and coaches, a state-of-the-art training regimen and diet, considerable racing

experience, and exceptional natural talent are most important. Your strategy for winning would revolve around these key factors. And most likely your top competitors will all strategize and prepare similarly.

But what if we changed the scenario? Suppose that it is just six months before the Olympics, and you are going to compete in a sport that you've never done before. Your goal is still to become one of the standout athletes of the games. What would be your formula for success now? Can you even think of one? It's much harder, isn't it? The context of the first scenario is familiar. It is the standard approach to athletic competition. All contestants compete on the same factors, resulting in very tight, head-to-head races where winners are often decided by a fraction of a second. The second scenario by contrast presents a very unusual strategic challenge, one that appears impossible, or at least requires unconventional thinking to crack.

Here is the real-life connection. In the 2000 Sydney Olympic Games, a swimmer from Equatorial Guinea, Eric "the Eel"

Moussambani qualified to compete, not by meeting the stringent minimum time standard, but by winning a wild card entry. Such cards are randomly allocated to athletes from third-world countries who otherwise would have no chance to meet the competitive standards. The underlying intent is to make the Olympics a world-encompassing event.

Eric gained instant superstar status after flailing and splashing his way to an improbable finish in a preliminary heat. After being exposed to a full-size swimming pool for the first time, and uninitiated in the complexity of a diving start, he still somehow managed to finish the one-hundred-meter heat to the spectators' uproarious reception. His courageous display of dilettantism—of doing his best against all odds—made him the sensation of the games and won worldwide attention, media invitations, and attractive promotional offers.

Imagine how you would feel if you won a gold medal in swimming with a terrific new world record time in the same event in which Eric swam his heat. You get up excitedly the next morning to look in the newspapers for the coverage of your glorious victory. You are rightfully expecting to receive front-page mention, due recognition for a crowning achievement of a lifetime of extreme dedication and hard work. But to your dismay the front page of every newspaper is plastered instead with the story and image of Eric, a guy who can't even swim. Your story has slipped to page six as a mere footnote. Has the world gone mad? What is going on?

What indeed? Why such raving public reaction for the worst swimmer in Olympic history? It is because Eric unintentionally sidestepped head-on competition against his infinitely more qualified rivals, and instead he gave spectators what they ultimately wanted: inspirational entertainment. And he accomplished this with minimal cost and investment. Eric, by default, eliminated using all the traditional key factors of his competitors that he had no access

to (intensive training, world-class coaching, standout facilities). Eric only learned to swim six months before the Olympics. His differentiating factors of competition were his big heart and unwavering effort. Among superhuman athletes who seemed almost in a world of their own and untouchable, Eric was refreshingly ordinary, allowing consumers to immediately identify with him. To them his story felt fully relevant. So Eric came to inadvertently personify the very essence of Blue Ocean Strategy: make the competition irrelevant by offering superior consumer value (inspirational entertainment) at a lower cost (by doing without the traditional factors of competition) in a way that ignites mass appeal. Multitudes of people around the world who ordinarily would not be interested in sports were suddenly drawn to the Olympics because of Eric's saga.

Along the way, Eric also happened to accomplish the other key directives outlined in this book—infatuate consumers, provide them with an enriching experience, and transcend the traditional boundaries of what you can offer them. From an ill-equipped Olympic athlete to a beacon of inspiration. Way to go, Eric!

Alas, I have another riddle for you. Are you ready? How can french fries save the world and lead you to Blue Oceans?

Allow me to rephrase the question. What would you say if you were a leading fast-food company with the prospect of achieving a combination of powerful sensory branding, a massive environmentally friendly image boost, and the ability to turn waste into a prominent complementary offering? Does this seem too good to be a feasible Value Innovation move? Well, it may not be as far-fetched as you think.

Vegetable oil is a viable (although not yet practical) source of automobile fuel. Joshua Tickell gained visibility for its use in 1997, when he drove his Veggie Van across the United States by using leftover vegetable oil from Kentucky Fried Chicken and other fast-food chains. Vegetable oil can be used in converted diesel engines.

In America alone, there are 4.5 billion gallons (18 billion liters) of vegetable oil waste generated every year by restaurants, which has to be collected and removed. So there lies the opportunity: instead of getting rid of this waste, why not convert it into an eco-friendly fuel source via add-on fuel pumps at fast-food outlets? The retail network infrastructure is already in place, and motorists and cars can both tank up together via the drive-through! A car manufacturer could be partnered with the fast-food outlets to produce the vegetable oil–powered cars. Here's the kicker: exhaust from a car burning vegetable oil gives off a pleasant, nearly irresistible french fry smell, continuously luring everyone to fast-food restaurants. Thus the infatuation of consumers

and the Value Innovation scenario itself is complete, and a vast Blue Ocean awaits!

Saved for last is something more tangible. Perhaps you have recently visited one of the Disney theme parks around the world and gotten to experience their Fastpass system. The Fastpass is simply an online reservation system that allows visitors to design their in-park itinerary prior to their arrival. By doing so, they can circumvent waiting in line at the park. It's like having a reserved seat for a flight rather than going standby. The Fastpass is a free service for visitors. On the surface, it doesn't seem like a big deal. Or does it? Because why would a Disney executive go so far as to say that the deployment of the Fastpass will have a deep, industry-wide impact?

At first glance the Fastpass seems trivial, nothing too distinctive, innovative, or influential. But what about its impact? What possible watershed does it simultaneously unlock for Disney and its consumers? For the answer, let's turn to Seth Godin's *Fast Company* column from December 19, 2007:

> *After 40 years of making people stand in line (lots of lines) at its parks, Disney woke up and instituted Fastpass, which allows visitors to reserve a spot in line and eliminate the wait. An astonishing 95% of its visitors like the change. "We have reinvented how to visit a park," Disney VP Dale Stafford told a reporter. "We have been teaching people how to stand in line since 1955, and now we are telling them they don't have to. Of all the things we can do and all the marvels we can create with the attractions, this is something that will have profound influence on the entire industry."*

So now one part of the Blue Ocean equation is clear: the exceptional enrichment that this seemingly simple tweak to Disney's core offering brings to consumers. Up until the Fastpass, everyone assumed that waiting in line was an immovable part of the overall experience. People heretofore spent an overwhelming portion of their time waiting in line, and this was the subject of most visitor complaints. For over forty years nothing was really done about it. Everyone operated within the traditional boundaries without challenging the conventional wisdom. With the arrival of the Fastpass, however, visitors' wait times were cut to a fraction, allowing them to have a profoundly more enjoyable experience. But how about the other part of the equation, that of simultaneously achieving lower costs?

To see this clearly, we should look at Disney's approach to innovation. In a Red Ocean state of mind, theme parks are in a savage race to boast their most thrilling rides. They want to be known as "the" park with the highest or the fastest roller coaster. For example, one of Disney's recent big splashes was the Mission: Space motion simulator thrill ride at Epcot, which opened in 2003 at an estimated development cost of $100 million. But of course Disney's competitors—such as Six Flags, Universal Studios, and Lego Land—didn't stand still. Each is investing massive amounts of capital in order to win the coveted title of having the most thrilling ride, resulting in incremental and fleeting distinction at staggering costs. This race has gotten so intense that the rides are now scraping the limits of human physiology. Two people with preexisting conditions died from riding on Mission: Space, and many others have gotten quite ill. So potential next steps along this innovation dimension are getting to be prohibitively limited and expensive.

Wired magazine regularly asks its readers to use their imagination and project what various offerings might look like in the future. Here is one submission regarding the projected evolution and functionality of amusement park rides in the year 2019, echoing my observations above: "In the event of a life-threatening arrhythmia, resuscitation equipment embedded in the ride will send a direct, therapeutic jolt of electricity."

In contrast to the $100 million spent on Mission: Space, how much would you guess that the Fastpass reservation system cost? A mere fraction, at most. Yet it was this innovation that unlocked the most persistent and significant barrier to a more enriching consumer experience. How? But wait, there's more! Even though the Fastpass is free, it allows Disney to increase its revenues and profitability on several levels. First, since visitors have more time to spend on having fun rather than waiting in line, they will have more opportunities to spend money on food, drinks, and souvenirs. Park entrance fees can also be more justifiably increased. And Disney parks can now attract a previously untapped, massive consumer segment: all the people who before would never consider visiting because of the excessive waiting. For them, when trying to decide the best way to spend the next family vacation, Disney now surfaces for the first time as a viable option. So in this sense the entire industry benefits, with lifestyle driving implications.

Notice how all facets of Value Innovation are again represented here. In this case they are centered around a small adjustment to the core offering of a long-standing business with disproportionately big results. Of course the Fastpass cannot remain a differentiator for long, because it can be copied easily by competitors. But if they do copy it, the entire theme park industry as a whole will become more appealing to consumers. And in true Blue Oceanographer frame of mind, Disney should already be on its next impactful move. **Because creating Blue Oceans is never about a one-time illumination but a continuous process of discovery.**

Let's now tie this example back to the Accordion Chart, remembering that insights from the chart form the basis for actionable Blue Ocean strategies. How would constructing an Accordion Chart lead to the idea of the Fastpass? As its core utility, Disney is a theme park, but a broader view sees it as a family entertainment destination. By simply elevating our focus from within the narrow confines of theme parks—where competition is based on boasting the newest and fastest rides—to that of family entertainment destinations, we would recognize that an important dimension in that broader space (shared by such other destinations as beachside resorts, tourist-magnet cities, animal safaris, and ski resorts) is the ability to entertain consumers for the entirety of their visit and not just for intermittent bursts. This is the key insight that led to the introduction of the Fastpass, and it is one that the visual mapping of an Accordion Chart helps to identify.

The story of the Fastpass demonstrates how the long-established core business of a company can be galvanized by the application of Accordion Chart and Value Innovation perspectives. To round out my tale of Disney, let's consider an example of how Disney is fabricating new offshoots from its core business. Taken together, the two Disney illustrations show how the Accordion Chart and Value Innovation mind-set can be harnessed both for continuously tweaking your core business as well as finding new frontiers of consumer relevance. Both fine-tuning and redefining your core business in this manner can result in the discovery of Blue Oceans.

The complementary example is Disney's foray into designing hospitals. On the surface this may seem like a stretch. What does Disney know about designing hospitals? What relevant know-how can they possibly contribute? However, when viewed through the Accordion Chart perspective, it doesn't seem too farfetched. As its core utility, Disney is a theme park. More generally defined, it is a family entertainment destination. If we expand the definition even further, we could say that Disney is in the business of making people have fun, feel good, and enjoy life. Therein lies the connection. Being in an environment that makes them feel good is exactly what patients in hospitals need to help accelerate their recovery and improve their treatment experience, which suddenly makes Disney's design expertise highly relevant.

Disney helped design the University of Colorado Hospital's $145 million Anschutz Inpatient Pavilion in the suburbs of Denver. *USA Today* reported:

> *At a theme park, they tap fun. In hospitals, they cope with fear. And in the end, Colorado officials found that it doesn't cost more to treat patients like guests. At $1,120, a night's stay at the new hospital costs the same as it did at the old one. But the difference is dramatic.*
>
> *There are subtle elements of theater throughout the hospital, where Disney designers consider*

staff members "on stage" when they interact with patients. Downstairs, as the hospital door slides open, music from a grand piano mixes with Mile High sunshine streaming into the lobby. At the curb, the valet parking is free. Inside the lobby, employees are cheerful and friendly, and no one is wearing white coats or surgical scrubs.

Everything in the University of Colorado Hospital's design was judged based on how it makes the patient feel. The Disney team put planners in wheelchairs, both literally and virtually, so that they could see the hospital from the patient's perspective.

There you have it. The hospital design expertise that Disney provides as an offshoot of its core business is highly relevant, lifestyle enriching, and market driving. It also encapsulates Value Innovation. How might that be again? Notice first that in this instance the price is set high ($1,120 per night per patient) to strategically match that of the industry. Value Innovation comes from breaking the mold of how to maximize patient value at this price point. The shift in perspective from treating consumers as patients to treating them as guests leads to the reallocation of design and operational resources from those that provide a purely clinical experience to 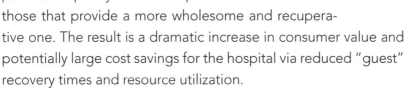 those that provide a more wholesome and recuperative one. The result is a dramatic increase in consumer value and potentially large cost savings for the hospital via reduced "guest" recovery times and resource utilization.

What are the overall takeaways in terms of strategy and business application?

1 Blue Ocean Strategy is a systematic framework for transforming unconventional ideas into successful strategies. Using insights from Accordion Charts as the foundation for the application of Blue Ocean Strategy enables you to formulate market driving strategies that achieve lifestyle enrichment and continued relevance.

2 Blue Oceans are the vast market spaces beyond conventional frontiers, where the simultaneous pursuit of lower cost and differentiation leads to new demand creation. This duality of Value Innovation is based on the reallocation of resources from those factors that add little or no consumer value to an offering to those that heighten consumer relevance. This approach puts you in a position to maximize your business success and market impact. Inspiration and examples are all around you. Take note that often trivial and seemingly insignificant moves are the ones that unlock the greatest impact simply because no one else has challenged taken-for-granted assumptions, as with the Disney Fastpass.

3 In contrast, Red Oceans are bound by limitations of conventionality that gobble up resources in head-to-head competition and endanger the strategic relevance of companies engaged in it. In Red Oceans, a single penny can put you out of business, and the biggest can sink the fastest.

4 Economic upheaval and market frivolity further increase the imperative of creating Blue Oceans, because unprecedented times call for unconventional measures. Furthermore, searching for Blue Oceans allows you to avoid blindly slashing costs in favor of reallocating resources in a way that provides the basis for continued growth. If given the choice, wouldn't you want to see the marketplace full of limitless possibilities rather than full of looming dangers? That choice is yours for the taking.

In the next chapter I present a bouquet of real-life examples. Each shows the full application of the interrelated concepts set forth to this point.

The Slingshot Framework

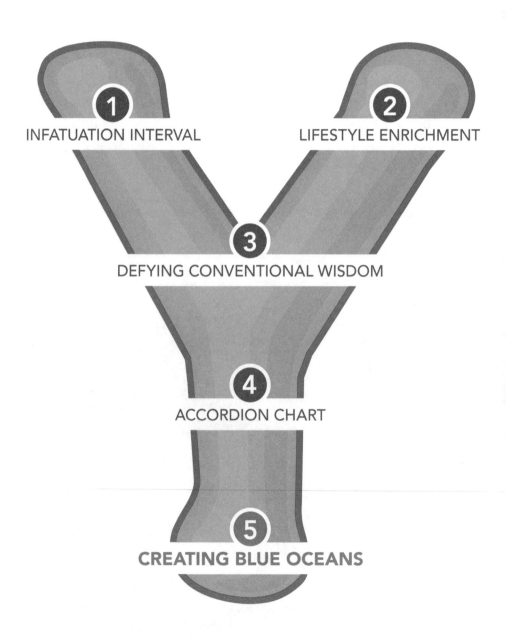

Have you visited **www.slingshotliving.com** lately?
If not, you're missing half the fun and learning.

PROOF OF THE PUDDING 6

The proof of the pudding is the eating.

—Fourteenth-Century Proverb

It is now time for action. How do the interlocking concepts presented in the previous chapters hold up in real life? I will now offer tangible examples. These range from those I have observed and studied to those I have helped to create and those I have originated. As you read through each case, look for supportive proof for what has been discussed. Ask yourself the following questions, which I will address at the end of each story:

1 Are consumers being infatuated?

2 Does the offering create lifestyle enrichment?

3 Does it overstep traditional boundaries and challenge conventional wisdom in a way that is market driving?

4 Does the Accordion Chart reveal that the offering achieves a broader, more encompassing consumer utility and relevance?

5 Does it embody Value Innovation as defined by Blue Ocean Strategy?

I shall begin with the story of Dr. Seuss, whom I have referenced and quoted several times throughout the book. And for a very good reason: Theodor Geisel, the creator of the Dr. Seuss children's book series, is a wonderful example of the entire chain of concepts presented here. His stories and characters redefined a whole segment of the book industry and significantly grew its target audience in the process. Here is how he did it. In the 1950s so-called primers or early readers—books designed to teach children in the United States to read—could only contain the 223 frequently used words approved by an official reading list (called the Dolch word list).

One example of such children's books is the Dick and Jane series, which by the 1950s an estimated 80 percent of first graders were using in the United States. Here's a short excerpt from one of the Dick and Jane books:

> **"I see my blue car.**
> **I see my yellow car.**
> **Look, Father, look.**
> **Find my little red car."**

Not surprisingly the books were rather boring and unimaginative and hence did not really inspire youngsters to read. Using the same 223 words, Geisel broke the mold completely because he did not see them as limitations but rather as building blocks for his Dr. Seuss stories. He set out to combine the best of what early readers had (simplicity) and that of another major category of children's books (the entertaining story and moral message elements of traditional fairy tales), and added his trademark zany humor, rhyme, and illustrations to the mix. As a result, he created timeless books that not only kids but adults love to read. The first in this series was *The Cat in the Hat* published in 1955, when the author was at the tender age of fifty-one. It tells the story of an outrageously naughty cat that unexpectedly shows up to entertain a pair of siblings who are home alone on a rainy day. Even though it uses only the simplified vocabulary of the Dolch word list, it succeeds in hooking readers right from the start.

> **"The sun did not shine.**
> **It was too wet to play."**
> **–and so the classic tale begins.**

How does Dr. Seuss measure up to the questions we asked above? Let's take a look.

Are Consumers Being Infatuated?

Absolutely! Dr. Seuss created stories that grabbed the imagination of children to such an extent that they still love to read them as adults. That is an astonishing, lifelong infatuation.

Does the Offering Create Lifestyle Enrichment?

It sure does. Giving kids a means to enjoy the process of learning to read is an empowering enrichment that will have a cascading, positive effect on their subsequent education. And having stories that entertainingly pack a moral message continue to enrich their lives as grown-ups.

Does It Overstep Traditional Boundaries and Challenge Conventional Wisdom in a Way That Is Market Driving?

While all constituents involved (writers, kids, parents, teachers) accepted the existing limitations, namely, that the strict official reading list negated the possibility of creating both enjoyable and educational children's books, Dr. Seuss did not. He overstepped this perceived boundary and drove the market in a new direction. In doing so, Dr. Seuss personified the power of rediscovering our childhood imagination. He fabricated his stories in a way that kids could easily relate to them. In other words, he was able to reconnect with his own childlike creativity to defy convention—just look at the quote at the top of chapter 3 for the source of his inspiration. Second, his books allow adults, even if briefly or occasionally, to reclaim their buried youth, which is the basis for their timeless popularity.

Does the Accordion Chart Reveal That the Offering Achieves a Broader, More Encompassing Consumer Utility?

The narrowest definition of utility for Dr. Seuss's books is still early readers: books designed to teach kids to read. But he was not satisfied to compete strictly within this narrow segment. Instead, he elevated his books to the much broader utility of educational entertainment by combining the best elements of traditionally separate offerings and adding new ones of his own. As with all the examples that follow, a simplified Accordion Chart for Dr. Seuss is displayed here, showing the enlargement of consumer utility from its most narrow definition to its most broad.

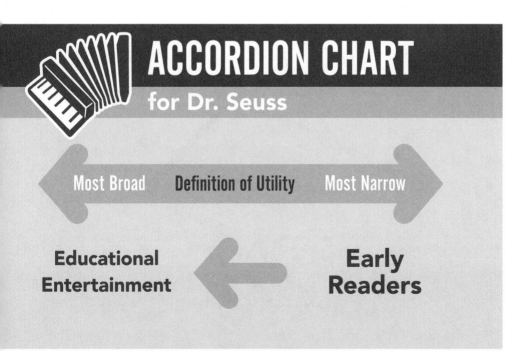

ACCORDION CHART
for Dr. Seuss

Most Broad   Definition of Utility   Most Narrow

Educational
Entertainment

Early
Readers

Does the Offering Embody Value Innovation as Defined by Blue Ocean Strategy?

Using the visual tool set of Blue Ocean Strategy, the Value Innovation of Dr. Seuss is depicted in the **strategy canvas** below. Each subsequent example will also feature a strategy canvas, which lists the most important factors of competition for a given market space along the horizontal axis of the chart, and then depicts the relative levels of key players across them. These relative levels represent the comparative investment or emphasis among key competitors, or their resource allocation, which in turn define the strategic positioning of their offering toward consumers. The canvas here uses a basic scale of 0 to 3 to portray players' positioning on each factor of competition (0 meaning

The "Fantastical" Value Innovation of Dr. Seuss

Target audience: children learning to read

● Fairy Tales   ● Early Reader books in the 50's   ● Dr. Seuss Stories

Story Complexity · Moral Message · Entertainment · Educational · Zany Humor nonexistent, 1–low, 2–medium, 3–high). By connecting the points across factors for each player, we can depict their **value curve**, indicating their relative value proposition toward consumers. The visual simplification of the strategy canvas (showing only the top players, the most important factors of competition, and a basic scale) allows for a clear focus on the core dynamics of a market space. Simplifying complex things in a way that they can make sense and provide insights is a wonderful throwback to child-hood thinking.

The strategy canvas for Dr. Seuss clearly illustrates the compelling new market space he created. His value curve is a combination of the best attributes from two traditionally separate, alternative offerings. Fairy tales had high complexity, moral message, and entertainment value, but they were usually read to children by parents. Hence they were not really an education tool to help kids learning to read, which is the type of educational value we are after here. Fairy tales are certainly educational in passing down collective wisdom, which on this chart is shown as moral message. In contrast, early readers were educational, very simple, but without much moral or entertainment value. As depicted by Dr. Seuss's value curve, his stories eliminated the complexity of fairy tales while retaining much of their moral message and matching their entertainment value. At the same time, his stories raised the educational value of early readers to unprecedented levels and added the new dimension of zany humor and illustrations. The resulting offering created clear differentiation with lower cost (eliminating story complexity), and greatly expanded market demand (among both children and adults)—hence Value Innovation.

Think here of the parallels to Dan Brown and *The Da Vinci Code* cited earlier: Dan Brown was able to repackage the central theme of a previous book, much like Dr. Seuss was able to recycle the words used by other children's authors before him in a way that unlocked mass appeal. While Dr. Seuss was neither the most outstanding illustrator nor the best poet of his time, his books transformed the way children learned to read and remain cross-generational favorites for more than half a century. Therein lies the empowering shift in strategic focus: you don't need to be the best at what you do as long as you can be the most relevant. In other words, the recipe for success is not to strive to be the best by any traditional measure. **Rather, the path of least resistance is to sidestep traditional measures and to aim instead for maximum relevance to consumers.**

Coincidentally, the very first Dr. Seuss book, *To Think That I Saw It on Mulberry Street,* was rejected by twenty-nine publishers before it was finally accepted. Could it perhaps be that those publishers were all too grown-up to appreciate the true potential of Dr. Seuss's marvelous creations and sadly let him slip away?

Let's jump to something equally fun but contemporary. The Cow Parade successfully straddles the art, business, and social responsibility worlds while reinventing the concept of public art. Started in Chicago in 1999, its basic premise is to transform entire cities into art moo-seums. Here is the idea: take a bunch of life-size, fiberglass cow replicas and invite a variety of artists to custom decorate each one, and then disperse them throughout the downtown outdoor areas of designated cities for public viewing. To keep things simple, there are only three cow poses: standing, grazing, and reclining. Each year the exhibition is organized in four to five host cities around the world.

In the ten years since its inception, the Cow Parade has posted some hugely impressive stats: it has exhibited in over fifty major cities on six continents, drawn over one hundred million spectators, featured over five thousand artists, and raised over $20 million for charitable causes. Among former host cities are such cultural heavyweights as New York City, London, Tokyo, Istanbul, Buenos Aires, Sydney, Johannesburg, and Moscow. 2010 host cities included São Paulo, Rome, and Tunis.

Plain cows are painted and adorned by a diverse group of local artists, ranging from unknown amateurs to professionals and celebrities. Well-known personalities who have contributed designs for past shows include Ronnie Wood, Kate Spade, Vaclav Havel, David Lynch, and Christian Lacroix. On average, 75 to 150 cows are displayed at each exhibition, which typically lasts two to four months during the area's peak tourist season. When an event winds down, the cows are auctioned off, with the proceeds going to local charitable causes. What's your guess for the record auction price so far for one of the cows? Well, the highest price fetched to date for a single sculpture is $146,000 after the show in Dublin in 2003 for a mosaic-covered cow by renowned designer John Rocha. Among tastemakers who have purchased cows are Oprah Winfrey, Ringo Starr, Elton John, and Princess Firyal of Jordan. Simply put, in just ten years the Cow Parade has become the world's largest and most successful public art project. What is behind its success?

Perhaps like the circus before Cirque du Soleil, art exhibitions might have been on their way to obsolescence before the Cow Parade. Younger generations have too many diversions, too many entertainment options vying for their time to pay much attention to art museums. Once this trend is identified, we can see that the solution was not in tweaking the offering platform of traditional museums but by rethinking the very way art is displayed. That is exactly what the Cow Parade did. It did not seek new channels to attract consumers to museums but rather transformed cities themselves into museums.

With your indulgence, I would like to take a brief detour. Back in 2005, the following news blip appeared out of New York City:

> *In a reverse-theft of sorts, a British artist has been sneaking his works into some of New York's top museums.*
>
>
>
> **Banksy's "You have beautiful eyes," installed by the artist at the Met.**
>
> *The artist, who goes by the name Banksy, has surreptitiously hung works in the Metropolitan Museum of Art, the Museum of Modern Art, the American Museum of Natural History and the Brooklyn Museum.*
>
> *A self-described "career graffiti writer" and "painter-decorator," Banksy tells Michele Norris that he consulted biographies of Harry Houdini to get ideas about how to sneak into the museums with his artworks, some of which are not small at all.*
>
> *Asked why he carried out the pranks, Banksy says, simply: "I thought some of [the paintings] were quite good. That's why I thought, you know, put them in a gallery. Otherwise, they would just sit at home and no one would see them."*

Clearly, Banksy also perceived significant limitations in the way traditional museums operated and sought to defy conventional wisdom in search of a solution. However, in this case, he still accepted the physical confines of museums for displaying art, and as a result his initiative didn't quite have the broad vision and reach of the Cow Parade. It was a noteworthy effort nevertheless.

By daring to do something so bold, the Cow Parade created a compelling offering not just for the end consumer but for multiple other constituents alongside them.

For Host Cities:

By reconfiguring the entire city into an art exhibit, the Cow Parade makes art accessible to all who live there. Furthermore, it creates an international buzz that stimulates tourism and promotes the city's image as a progressive cultural center. Additionally, funds generated by the auction at the end of the event generate significant support for local charities.

For Artists:

The Cow Parade provides great exposure and some income ($1,000 per cow) for aspiring artists, a common platform to all local artists, and a vibrant connection between the local art and business communities.

For Corporate Sponsors:

Local companies have the opportunity to pick artists they want to sponsor from among those submitting designs. This allows companies to showcase their name next to the sculpture selected, resulting in a unique publicity display and customized artistic association.

For the Cow Parade Itself:

The events generate multiple revenue streams (sponsorship, merchandising, auction) along with a significant social activism component (reminiscent of Grameen Bank's combination of doing good business and doing good cited earlier), all in the form of an easily replicable business model with tremendous worldwide reach.

Are Consumers Being Infatuated?

Who can possibly resist a cow? They were purposely picked as the theme because of their benign and universally loved form. The emotional connection, of course, goes back to our childhood, when a cow was among the first animals whose image, name, and sound we learned to recognize. We also love cows for all things related to milk, and for their gentle, peaceful temperament. So, yes, the cows do provide an immediate source of infatuation.

But in this case the question of infatuation goes deeper. First, because we can talk about infatuation not just of the end consumer (the spectators) but of the other constituent groups as well. I contend that city organizers, participating artists, and even sponsoring companies are equally infatuated by being part of such a distinctive and uplifting event. Second, let's suppose that there are some surly, Grinch-like consumers who do not fall in love with the cows on display. For them, the event is just a big, disorderly nuisance. Still, they have no choice but to endure it and to walk past the cows every day during the exhibition on their way to work, the gym, the bank, or the coffee shop.

So, in this sense, the Cow Parade expands the definition of infatuation. By bringing its offering to be in continuous and unavoidable contact with a mass of consumers, even if some among them are not infatuated at first, they have no choice but to accept it as being part of their daily livies. For artists whose bovine designs are on display, any critical reaction to their work is preferred to no reaction. After all, the bane of art is not controversy but obscurity. Initially critical reaction to art, with a bit of time and familiarity, can turn into infatuation. The Eiffel Tower comes to mind immediately as a symbolic illustration. When first erected at the end of the nineteenth century, it was seen by many as a monstrous oddity piercing the classic skyline of Paris. But today, who could imagine the city without it? Who doesn't think of it as one of the most romantic and endearing monuments in the world?

Does the Offering Create Lifestyle Enrichment?

The Cow Parade creates both lifestyle and workstyle enrichment. The former is achieved for the city dwellers whose environment is enriched by the colorful pageantry of cows; likewise, tourists get to experience something special during their visit to the city. The latter is realized for participating artists, who get to conceive of and display their work in a meaningful new way.

Does It Overstep Traditional Boundaries and Challenge Conventional Wisdom in a Way That Is Market Driving?

The Cow Parade is hugely market driving, as evidenced by the statistics mentioned earlier. Overstepping, in fact, reversing conventional wisdom, it created a format where people don't go to art, but art goes to the people. It is reminiscent of Starbucks' market-driving effect in reversing the equation of people taking coffee to work to that of people taking work to cafés.

Does the Accordion Chart Reveal That the Offering Achieves a Broader, More Encompassing Consumer Utility?

In its strictest definition, the Cow Parade is an art exhibit. But by blowing off the doors and busting out from the confines of traditional museums, it elevates its offering to that of a citywide, continuous spectacle. By converting entire cities into moo-seums, it collapsed the utilities of several traditionally separate market segments, namely, citywide art projects, urban tourist attractions, fun outdoor destinations, and charitable fund-raising events.

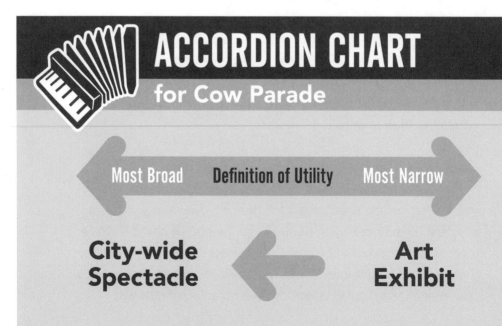

ACCORDION CHART
for Cow Parade

Most Broad   Definition of Utility   Most Narrow

City-wide Spectacle   Art Exhibit

Does the Offering Embody Value Innovation as Defined by Blue Ocean Strategy?

Take a look at the strategy canvas on the next page. What do you see? Even at first glance you can already tell that the Cow Parade's value curve is the opposite of that for a leading contemporary art exhibit in a museum. In comparing the two, the Cow Parade eliminated Venue Attraction and Artist Appeal—the two most important factors of competition for traditional art exhibits—driving cost savings. In other words, instead of spending significant resources to create the most striking indoor venue or to attract the single most desirable artist, the Cow Parade eliminated competing along these dimensions completely. It also eliminated the factor of Price, because its spectacle is free to the public.

As we move to the right of the canvas, we can see the other part of the Cow Parade strategy. By being continuously displayed in the open air, the Cow Parade became a twenty-four-hour art exhibit, doing away with another important limitation of traditional museums: Opening Hours. The combination of no visitor fees, twenty-four-hour access, and art coming to the people created total accessibility. It also raised the International Relevance and therefore touristic draw of the exhibition and created two new dimensions: Citywide Display and broad Variety of Artists. This complete reshuffling of the factors of competition resulted in value innovation: high differentiation, elimination of traditional, costly components, and a tremendous spike in demand among end-consumers as well as among multiple, supplementary constituent groups. And let's not forget the multiple revenue streams created in the form of auctions, accessories, and corporate sponsorship.

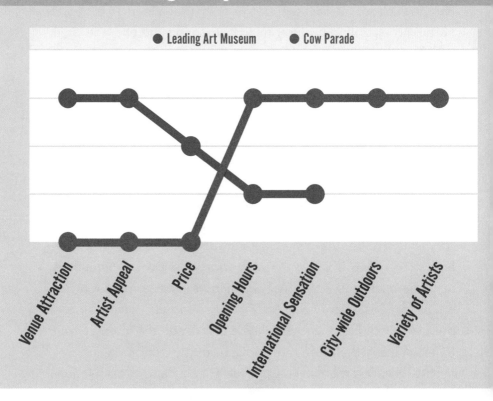

Big City – Contemporary Art Exhibit

"Turning a city into a moo-seum"

● Leading Art Museum   ● Cow Parade

Venue Attraction · Artist Appeal · Price · Opening Hours · International Sensation · City-wide Outdoors · Variety of Artists

Is there any child not captivated by speed and the idea of going as fast as possible? Are kids not in awe of the fastest cars they see? Are fast cars symbols of pure freedom, the ultimate embodiment of limitless possibilities? How many people dream of creating their own? This next case is about a boy who turned such a dream and fascination into a reality.

Supercars are the fastest and among the most expensive production cars made in the world. By most standards of measure, the realm of manufacturing them seems almost impossible to crack. It is dominated by a handful of iconic, long-established companies, such as Ferrari, Lamborghini, and McLaren, with rich traditions, considerable resources, and technical expertise. But still, if you wanted to make good on your childhood dream of making the world's best supercar, you would not let such obstacles derail you. Instead, you would rely on your childlike ingenuity to guide you.

The Fastest Car Ever

Thus unfolds the story of Swedish automotive maverick Christian von Koenigsegg. I met Christian in the spring of 2007 at a regional leadership event in Muscat, Oman, of all places, and I was captivated by his story. At five years old, Christian watched a cartoon about a bicycle repairman who built a racecar, and his life goal was formulated then and there. In 1994, the twenty-two-year-old Christian sprang into action. These were the assumptions he had to challenge, the traditions he had to overstep in order to realize his dream:

- Supercars can only be built by large, established companies.
- There could be no better or faster car than the McLaren F1, which at the time held the speed record for supercars.

- A long body shape is needed for the car to achieve maximum speed.
- A very large engine must be used.
- It is not possible to further reduce aerodynamic drag on a road car for higher speed and power level (tellingly reminiscent of the claim that the human body was not designed to run faster than a four-minute mile before Roger Bannister debunked it in 1954).

Christian did not see any of these limitations as set in stone, but rather waiting to be challenged. With neither extensive engineering experience nor unlimited financing (but about $2.5 million of family money), he set to it. Within ten years he achieved his dream and conquered the title as the maker of the fastest production car in the world. Along the way, he was joined by a group of diverse experts spurred on by a shared dream and the necessity to harness the furthest reaches of their collective creativity to make do with limited resources.

Here is a brief chronology of Koenigsegg Auto AB:

1994: Company launched by Christian von Koenigsegg with the dream of creating the fastest and best supercar

1995: In only one and a half years, a fully operational prototype was ready

2000: Series production starts

2004: Introduction of CCR model: "A car that leaves all others behind"

2005: CCR sets new speed record, overtaking the McLaren F1, at 241 mph (388 km/h)

2007: CCXR becomes world's first green supercar, running on biofuel and generating over 1,000 horsepower

2009: A consortium of investors led by Koenigsegg is set to acquire Saab from GM but later withdraws its offer

Amazingly, the company still operates out of a former air force base near Angelholm, Sweden, with only a few dozen full-time staff. Notice that Koenigsegg not only set the new speed record, but it also made the first "green" supercar. In the summer of 2009 Christian and a group of investors agreed to acquire Saab from General Motors, to bring the storied car company back under Swedish ownership. With months of delays in gaining regulatory approval and finalizing the acquisition, Koenigsegg opted out of the deal in December, because timeliness was paramount in trying to resurrect the loss-making company. Still, the incident made clear that Christian's influence is already well beyond supercars and reverberates throughout the automotive industry. Not bad for a boy with a seemingly impossible dream.

Are Consumers Being Infatuated?

There can be little debate that supercars are instruments of pure infatuation. They are the toys of the superrich, with a price range of several hundred thousand dollars to a couple of million. But Christian von Koenigsegg broke into this market segment in a way that provided even more infatuation, even more reasons for the superrich to feel giddy. He created the fastest supercar and the first green supercar and also redefined the emotional connection between car owner and manufacturer. In Christian's view, traditional supercar manufacturers were hiding too much behind their brand. They became too faceless and impersonal, and they no longer directly connected to the personalities of their founders. As an alternative, he wanted to show a close, personal connection between himself as the inventor and his cars to "give more soul to the product." It is this kind of direct connection and story that car aficionados find fascinating and get even more infatuated about.

Does the Offering Create Lifestyle Enrichment?

Besides the sheer joy of driving the world's fastest production car (a possibly fleeting title), Koenigsegg provides additional dimensions of enrichment. His cars are beautifully designed. In 2008, *Forbes* magazine voted the CCXR as one of the ten most beautiful cars of all time. Furthermore, their unique design gives the cars an explosion of additional lifestyle enriching qualities within the supercar market:

1 A no frills, function-based design that is still beautiful.

2 Best power-to-weight ratio.

3 Shortest braking
distance.

4 Highest
cornering G's.

5 Largest and most ergonomic
interior space.

6 Largest luggage space
(some competitors do not have any).

7 Highest passenger
safety.

8 Integrated hardtop that is storable in the car. With the
hardtop, the cars are a full coupe with no drawback in
shape or function. Basically two cars in one.

9 Low production volume
ensures exclusivity.

Does It Overstep Traditional Boundaries and Challenge Conventional Wisdom in a Way That Is Market Driving?

Take a look at the list on the previous page of the imposing assumptions that Christian faced and challenged when he decided to manufacture a supercar. In addition, what he succeeded in creating in terms of the total package of new capabilities was absolutely market driving for a supercar.

Does the Accordion Chart Reveal That the Offering Achieves a Broader, More Encompassing Consumer Utility?

By definition, supercars are a rather narrow market segment whose core utility is speed and performance. Even so, Christian was able to broaden his cars' utility and infuse them with dimensions that were not traditionally associated with supercars, such as safety, comfort, and practicality. In this way he expanded the utility of the cars for target consumers, who could now buy a supercar not just to own but to drive frequently and enjoy more. In addition, he created relevance for his cars among previous

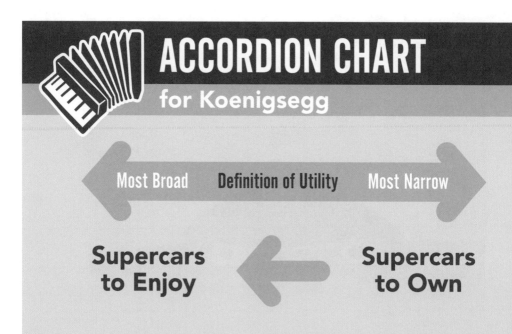

nonconsumers, who albeit rich were formerly put off by the limited functionality of supercars.

Does the Offering Embody Value Innovation as defined by Blue Ocean Strategy?

The strategy canvas on the next page shows the value curve of Koenigsegg vs. McLaren. Notice that price is not listed among the key factors of competition. This is because the supercar market segment has more important dimensions than price, as consumers tend to be fairly price insensitive. At first glance, look at how intimidating the value curve of McLaren appears on its own. It scores high pretty much across all traditional criteria. Trying to outcompete makes no sense for a newcomer with limited resources. Echoing the story above, Christian eliminated the factors of competition that he deemed superfluous, such as Styling, Brand, and Tradition. He knew that he could not compete with a McLaren or Ferrari on the appeal of brand and tradition, and he did not want to compete with them on styling—which he saw as an impediment to performance.

He believed that simplicity, not ornamentation, would provide the car's design appeal. Image remained an important factor to cultivate, but one where, in the beginning at least, he would lag behind the other players. So he turned up the heat on two other key factors (Performance and Exclusivity) and created two new ones for supercars (Personality—which he defined as "having a soul," a strong connection between the inventor and the car itself—and Functionality). The resulting combination created clear differentiation at lower cost as Christian was able to focus entirely on delivering the best driving experience to consumers, which in turn grew the number of potential consumers. *Forbes* magazine noted: "The Koenigsegg CCX, the all-new, exotic Swedish supercar, performs like the Bugatti, at about half the price. Yet with less than 20 cars available annually in the U.S., some say it's destined to be more coveted because it's within reach of a much larger pool of the rich and famous."

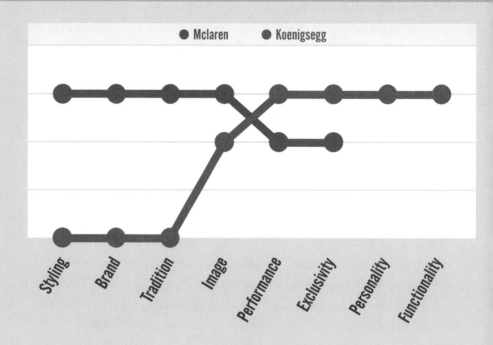

Reinventing Supercars: Koenigsegg vs. McLaren

"A car that leaves all others behind"

● Mclaren   ● Koenigsegg

Styling Brand Tradition Image Performance Exclusivity Personality Functionality

Let's stay within the car industry for our next example, but let's swing all the way to its other extreme. This way we see how meaningful innovation, based on unconventional thinking, is possible at both ends of a mature industry. This story is about Tata Motors of India.

Tata Motors set out to innovate at the bottom end of one of the oldest and most competitive industries: the automotive. In

March 2009 the company introduced the world's most affordable car, the Nano, with a retail price of $2,500. What Tata identi-
fied was a potentially huge untapped market—as many as one
hundred million people in India alone—who couldn't afford the
least expensive cars on the market (priced at around $5,000)
and instead drove their family around on a motorcycle (priced at
around $1,000). So Tata asked the question, How could a means
of transport be developed that would be appropriate and attractive for this consumer group?

The company then set out
to create a lifestyle-enriching
offering first by deciding
on an appropriate strate-
gic price, and then finding
innovative ways to make
it viable. It looked to consumer lifestyles for insights,
which allowed Tata to identify
expendable features such as a large engine
that would have been wasted on India's overcrowded streets
where average speed is less than 20 mph (33 km/h). It simplified
other dimensions, such as having only a single windshield wiper
(rather than the standard two) and doing away with the hatchback
door (the storage area can be accessed via the rear seats). None
of these measures detracted from the car's perceived utility by
target consumers. To further bring costs in line with the Nano's
strategic price, Tata instituted a new distribution system by which
the company shipped kits to be assembled at the point of sale by
dealers, cutting central assembly, distribution, and storage costs.
And the company worked closely from the project's inception
with principle suppliers such as Bosch from Germany and Delphi
from the United States to identify innovative solutions throughout
the supply chain.

All these steps defied industry norms and contributed to the financial viability of the Nano while upholding its key benefits for consumers. *Newsweek* magazine in February 2008 labeled the Nano part of the "new breed of 21st century cars" that exemplifies the "contrarian philosophy of smaller, lighter, cheaper." The Nano, when finished, was able to keep to the targeted strategic price point, boast exceptional fuel efficiency (over 50 mpg for city driving, or 4.7 l/100 km) and exemplify eco-friendliness with low emissions. An electric version is expected to be in production in the near future. Within two weeks of its spring market debut, the Nano had received 200,000 orders.

Are Consumers Being Infatuated?

Because the Nano is a new offering to the market, it's too early to tell. Admittedly, a Koenigsegg is easier to get infatuated about than a Nano. And I am sure the Nano will have its growing pains, given its bold mission. Still, I think its chances are pretty good. Given the car's affordability and overall features, a whole new mass of consumers will have access to a very capable car for the first time, which is a dream come true for many. That should be cause for infatuation.

Does the Offering Create Lifestyle Enrichment?

The Nano is symbolic of India's economic growth and upward mobility, which makes it highly relevant. It brings car ownership within reach of a large segment of its population, enabling consumers to personally experience the country's growing prosperity, which is deeply enriching to their lives.

Does It Overstep Traditional Boundaries and Challenge Conventional Wisdom in a Way That Is Market Driving?

Both the Nano's development process and package of attributes defy automotive conventionality. The sheer fact that Tata was able to create the world's most affordable car without eliminating any consequential features is market driving. So is the fact that it was able to identify a substantial and previously overlooked and underserved consumer group within one of the most mature industries. In large part due to the Nano, the Tata Group has been prominently recognized on *BusinessWeek*'s Top 100 list of the world's most innovative companies (number six in 2008 and number thirteen in 2009).

Does the Accordion Chart Reveal That the Offering Achieves a Broader, More Encompassing Consumer Utility?

While the Nano is undeniably a diminutive city car at its core, Tata expanded the definition of its utility to something much more encompassing: family transport. By doing so, Tata was able to gain critical insights into the lifestyle parameters of a large, previously marginalized consumer group and create an offering that would best satisfy it.

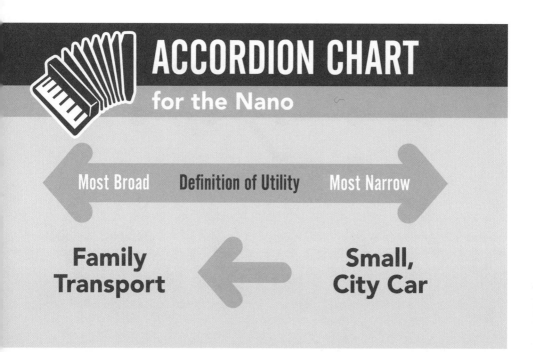

Does the Offering Embody Value Innovation as Defined by Blue Ocean Strategy?

In the strategy canvas below for budget cars, the value curve of an average budget car is pegged at a medium level for all factors. In contrast, Nano's value curve reinforces the mix of actions and strategic moves I have outlined: eliminating competing on factors deemed irrelevant, such as Engine Power (which drives cost savings). Tata strategically lowered Price and Size, raised Fuel Efficiency and Emission Standards, and created the new dimension of Simplicity to drive differentiation. In an overly complex world, injecting simplicity as a key factor of competition helps to create mass appeal. This is especially the case when going down

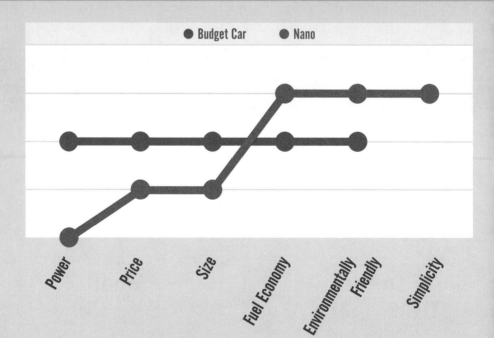

Reinventing Budget Cars in India: The Nano
"The people's car"

● Budget Car   ● Nano

Power   Price   Size   Fuel Economy   Environmentally Friendly   Simplicity

market as the Nano is doing, where simplicity is seen as a value enhancer while stripped-down is a value detractor.

Notice the stark contrast between the successful value curve of the Nano and that of Koenigsegg in the previous example. There isn't a single factor of competition that appears on both strategy canvases. While for the Nano, price was considered the key strategic enabler toward a new target consumer group, for Koenigsegg it was not one of the key differentiators. Taken together, the two cars demonstrate how the same strategic mind-set of unconventional thinking can lead you down very different paths and be successfully applied at both extremes of the auto industry. And if this can be done in the auto industry, why not in any other?

Back in 2003, AkzoNobel, the world's largest paint manufacturer, had a strategic challenge on its hands in Hungary. The Dutch company's local subsidiary was number two in the local market with a 20 percent market share and behind market leader Trilak, who was above 40 percent. Frustratingly, there was seemingly nothing that AkzoNobel could do to close the gap. In fact, its market share was declining while that of Trilak was on the rise.

That is when I met Peter de Groot, managing director of AkzoNobel Hungary. Peter was receptive to exploring unconventional approaches to crack his strategic quandary. We organized a two-day session involving his leadership team and set out to make use of the Accordion Chart and Value Innovation frameworks. The workshop took participants outside the traditional mental boundaries of their business and generated fresh insights and possibilities. The company shifted strategic direction as a result, and the market reaction was impressive. As this excerpt from *Business Hungary Magazine* explains:

In 2003, de Groot and his staff mapped out a business plan that was focused not on beating its competition, but on creating new market space that made the competition "irrelevant." De Groot made a controversial and prescient decision. "We decided we would not focus on the professional market," he recalls. At face value, the decision was reckless—professional painters are the industry's main customer base.

But de Groot and his team saw that Hungary's home-improvement industry was changing. More and more people were doing their own renovating, and even those homeowners who hired professional painters usually went to the paint store themselves to pick out colors and buy the products. "So we targeted the actual customer or end user," says de Groot.

The results were better than de Groot ever imagined. By reducing brands, simplifying the product, honing the message to appeal to do-it-yourselfers, and promoting environmentally friendly water-based paints, AkzoNobel appealed to its new customer base and rose to record sales levels and a commanding number one position in the woodcare market. As a result of this turnaround, de Groot was promoted to lead the corporation's international marketing arm.

In the year following the workshop, the company's sales grew 14 percent nationwide while that of Trilak remained stagnant. Now that's making some serious headway where previously none seemed possible.

Are Consumers Being Infatuated?

In AkzoNobel's new approach, they are no longer just selling paint to consumers via an intermediary, which was hardly cause for infatuation. What they are selling instead is a platform for consumer self-expression, empowering them directly to config- ure the color and texture com- binations of the living spaces inside their homes. Notice that in actuality the physi- cal product that the company sells has not changed at all. It is still paint. What has changed is the way it is shown, pack- aged, and communicated, which then shifts its percep- tion by consumers from some- thing mundane to something

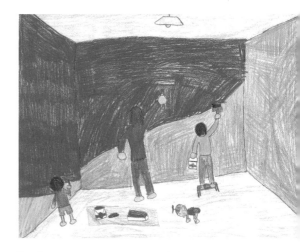

potentially captivating. As proof, the company was able to increase the price point of its paints as part of its new strategy, because consumers perceived additional value. So in a sense the change is minimal, but its effect is profound. Which is why every company should strive to reposition its offering in a way that it can be perceived by consumers as a source of infatuation.

Does the Offering Create Lifestyle Enrichment?

Reframing the context of their offering from that of a product to that of a platform of self-expression takes Peter's team away from thinking as a standard product supplier and enables it to think of itself as a lifestyle enrichment provider. The ensuing strategic steps demonstrated the new enriching qualities of AkzoNobel's reformulated offering, and the positive market reception was proof of its growing relevance.

Does It Overstep Traditional Boundaries and Challenge Conventional Wisdom in a Way That Is Market Driving?

The critical spark for the company's new strategy was its initial willingness to defy conventional industry wisdom. That in turn led AkzoNobel to redefine its target consumer from professional painters to end users, driving the do-it-yourself market in Hungary.

Does the Accordion Chart Reveal That the Offering Achieves a Broader, More Encompassing Consumer Utility?

Absolutely. How much more encompassing is the utility of self-expression than that of surface coatings? This question was brought into focus using the chart and was a key driver of the strategic shift taken. Building on this point, AkzoNobel's strategy not only encouraged consumers to select their own paint but also prompted them to apply it themselves, which broadened its offering's new utility even further to self-sufficiency (as a do-it-yourself enabler).

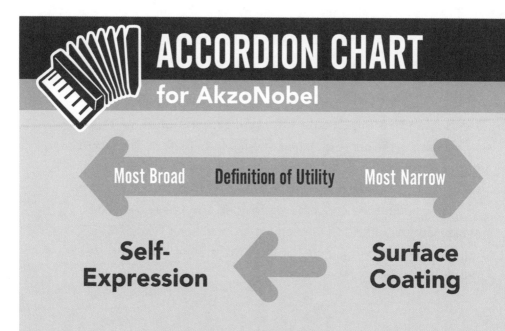

ACCORDION CHART
for AkzoNobel

Most Broad   Definition of Utility   Most Narrow

Self-Expression   Surface Coating

AkzoNobel: Re-thinking Paint

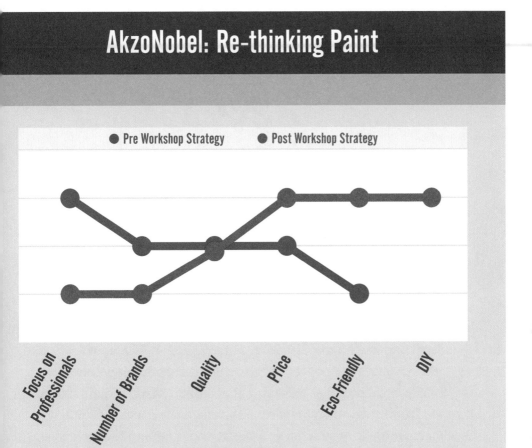

- ● Pre Workshop Strategy
- ● Post Workshop Strategy

Focus on Professionals · Number of Brands · Quality · Price · Eco-Friendly · DIY

Does the Offering Embody Value Innovation as Defined by Blue Ocean Strategy?

All three components of Value Innovation are here. The company shifted its focus away from professional painters, re-allocating resources from factors of competition that were not generating sufficient results. Peter's team was able to consolidate brands and simplify product lines, which led to cost savings while concurrently driving differentiation through the do-it-yourself message and eco-friendliness. The combination of these moves quickly unlocked new demand. By encouraging people to do their own home painting, the necessity of hiring a professional was removed, which meant that even though AkzoNobel raised the price point of its paints, the overall project cost to consumers was significantly reduced.

Razi Imam, the charismatic founder and CEO of Landslide Technologies, was on a mission: to crack open a very saturated market space. Iman was getting ready to launch his Pittsburgh-based company to contend against the likes of such giants as Oracle, Microsoft, SAP, and SalesForce.com in the crowded market space of sales force automation. That's like David deciding to go up against not one but a whole group of Goliaths at once.

In the fall of 2005, Iman secretly convened his fearless startup team and invited me to lead a strategy session that would evoke the powers of unconventional wisdom. I mentioned Landslide briefly in chapter 2 as an example of a B2B organization that created workstyle enrichment for consumers. Now let's look at their magic formula in a bit more detail. Without getting too technical, these are the initial goals that Landslide set for itself:

- We want Landslide to be known as the "Go To" company to solve sales issues.
- We want to be known as the company that offers process solutions for all complex sales situations.
- We want to be known as the best company to deliver sales-related services.
- We want to be known as the company owning the best content site powered by hundreds of expert authors and contributors.

There was certainly no shortage of solutions in the sales force automation market space before Landslide. However, they all seemed more process- than people-oriented, more focused on monitoring sales performance than improving it. This is what Landslide identified as the reigning tradition that was ripe to be challenged. The company set in motion the creation of an offering that would help salespeople sell like nothing before it. The above goals each aligned around this mission.

Once they got going, Iman's team uncovered so many possible differentiating dimensions to their offering that they had to restrain themselves and stagger their planned introduction so as not to overwhelm consumers, but to keep things simple and streamlined. That is a nice problem to have.

Right from the company's market entrance in 2006, Landslide was recognized by the Gartner Group (a leading provider of annual market research reports) as a "visionary" company within sales force automation. In fact, it is the only company to be identified as visionary every year since, even though the likes of Oracle, Microsoft, SAP, Siebel, and SalesForce.com are all competing in this industry.

On several occasions when I talked about Landslide during a presentation on strategy, participants came up to me afterward to tell me that they briefly visited the company's website on their handheld while I was speaking and were so impressed that they had already signaled colleagues via a quick e-mail to find out more. It's amazing how fast information is transmitted nowadays, especially relevant information. Landslide must really be on to something. Here is a sample client testimonial:

> *About 2 years ago, after working with many sales automation solutions that didn't seem to meet my company's needs, I was given the opportunity to begin utilizing the Landslide solution. Since moving to Landslide, I, as well as others on my sales team, have fully embraced the Landslide philosophy of Sales Workstyle Management, and I can honestly say that we have noticed a significant, positive change in the way we manage our client and prospective client opportunities.*
>
> *The Landslide solution has given me the ability to be more productive and strategic in my sales efforts, not to mention the fact that I can provide meaningful, real-time information to my manager and the executive team at TeleTracking. Not only am I a happy client/end-user, I take every opportunity possible to evangelize Landslide to friends and former co-workers at other organizations in hopes that they can make the advancement to Landslide.*
>
> —Bill Tedstrom, sales executive, TeleTracking

Are Consumers Being Infatuated?

You tell me. I think when a client testimonial includes the passage, "I take every opportunity to evangelize Landslide," there is a fairly good chance that there is some serious infatuation happening.

Does the Offering Create Lifestyle Enrichment?

More precisely, Landslide creates workstyle enrichment, enabling salespeople to have more meaningful work experiences: more effective, more comfortable, more fun.

Jill Konrath, author of *Selling to Big Companies,* commented, "Unless technology helps salespeople get business, they avoid it like the plague. That's why Landslide is so unique; sellers embrace it because it helps them win more sales and makes their job a whole lot easier at the same time."

Does It Overstep Traditional Boundaries and Challenge Conventional Wisdom in a Way That Is Market Driving?

Again, I will let market feedback speak for itself. Especially the one from the Gartner Group, which singled out Landslide as the only consistent visionary among its much bigger and more established market peers.

But Landslide is a good example of another characteristic of truly market-driving companies. Namely, their offering doesn't only blur traditional market boundaries but also becomes a balanced mix of product and service components. Remember how I said earlier that companies who can maintain a high level of relevance cease to think of themselves as product suppliers or service providers and instead think of themselves as being in the business of furnishing lifestyle enrichment. Companies that successfully blend product and service elements into one offering package are prime examples of this strategic shift. Consider how seamlessly iTunes and the iPod go together and are viewed as one meaningful package by consumers, even though one is a service and the other is a product. Similarly, Landslide combines elements of both: a software product with service components of secretarial support and continuous education.

Does the Accordion Chart Reveal That the Offering Achieves a Broader, More Encompassing Consumer Utility?

Iman's team could dig quite deep to pinpoint a very specific, technical definition of Landslide's core utility, but that is not the point. In fact, it is the trap that the other providers in this market segment fell into: they were too technical and process oriented. Instead, Landslide set out to help salespeople to sell, which represents a far broader utility. In pursuit of this, they blended elements from traditionally separate market segments—such as process software, sales performance tools, and personal sales assistance—all of which, once the target utility is elevated to helping salespeople sell, go naturally together, as revealed by the Accordion Chart.

Does the Offering Embody Value Innovation as Defined by Blue Ocean Strategy?

The strategy canvas below shows the value curve of Landslide against that of two major competitors, SalesForce.com and Siebel, as depicted by Iman's team. Note how similar the curves of the two competitors appear, visual proof that they are trying to outcompete each other on similar value propositions to consumers. They are seemingly caught in an escalating arms race. In contrast, Landslide occupies a distinctly separate market space. It withdrew

Landslide's Blue Ocean

● SalesForce.com   ● Siebel   ● Landslide

Tech Platform | Brand | CRM Functionality | Sales Process | Sales Tools | Buyer Collaboration | Sales Expertise | New Services (VIP)

itself from competing on trying to offer the very best Tech Platform or a highly recognized Brand and lowered its emphasis on pure CRM Functionality (monitoring of sales performance) as sources of cost savings. At the same time, Landslide pumped up Sales Process support, the variety of Sales Tools offered, and Collaboration with clients in designing their systems. It also created two new criteria— Sales Expertise (through its network of sales experts and online learning platforms) and access to New Services (including VIP, a twenty-four-hour sales assistance hotline)—in order to help increase sales performance and complete a well-differentiated, workstyle-enriching offering. Landslide created a veritable Blue Ocean.

As a reader of this book, chances are that at some point you have attended a seminar or speaking event on the topic of innovation, creativity, or motivation. I myself have participated in many. Even though most are held in wonderfully inspirational locations, with rare exceptions the actual presentations take place within the confines of blandly typical conference facilities. The result is that participants only get to enjoy the environment as an escape from the event—during breaks or designated free periods or, even worse, hardly at all. This has always struck me as contrarian and unfortunate. Wouldn't it make better sense to connect the message of the conference with the full motivational power of the surroundings rather than keep the two separate? This misses a golden opportunity to create a more profound and lasting impact and may even cause some resentment among participants for being teased with a great location without being able to fully enjoy it.

It seems that event organizers and participants both are stuck within the confines of self-imposed limitations, which is holding back fuller enrichment and wider consumer relevance. Think back to Disney's theme parks before the Fastpass.

This is why, whenever I have a say in the venue selection of an event I am part of, I push for a setting that complements and reinforces the topic and takeaway message. Sometimes this can happen spontaneously, such as convening on the beach or in the garden of a resort venue rather than in its conference facility. The consistent success of using such alternative settings led me to come up with the concept of a new learning platform entitled Immersive Executive Experience (IEE).

IEE is designed to be the harmonious combination of content and environment. It offers fully immersive, educational symposiums for business leaders and uses the backdrop of highly provocative environments as the classroom. It is designed to stimulate participants across all five senses and thereby generate experiential learning on such topics as recovering childhood creativity, defying conventional wisdom, and creating Blue Oceans of uncontested market space. The key driver here is that learning through doing, interactive idea-exchange, and absorption of one-of-a-kind experiences is far more meaningful than passively sitting through an indoor presentation. I know this statement seems self-evident, but why are most executive learning events still organized in ignorance of it? **An assertion can only be self-evident once someone dares to voice it.**

IEE locations are hand-picked, and they link client parameters with the appropriate level of environmental stimulation. Imagine holding a session on childhood creativity in a planetarium whose dome displays outer space as children fantasize it to look like. Or one on defying conventional wisdom while sitting around a mountain-top bonfire. Or on creating Blue Oceans while sailing on a catamaran.

Just as important as the setting are the reinforcing activities participants indulge in. Taking a boat ride along a saltwater marsh to witness mangrove trees thriving where conventional logic tells us that they have no business to do so—in an environment devoid of freshwater—can be mind-opening. Or teaming up with a couple of other participants not just to think about how the concept of fast food might be reinvented but to actually create a new prototype by cooking together. Or driving a racecar on a track and approaching the turn at such high speeds that your instincts are screaming for you to brake. But the racing instructor sitting next to you calmly signals for you to keep going full speed ahead, pushing you to successfully navigate the turn at a speed well beyond your perceived comfort zone. These types of experiences work to deeply internalize the application of unconventional thinking and to expand your habitual boundaries of exploration.

For an additional layer of experiential meaning, the sessions often create interaction with the local community itself. For example, as part of an IEE in a developing country like Belize, a local entrepreneur is assigned to each small group of executive participants. The task of the groups is to come up with an

actionable strategy for that entrepreneur's business idea (which may be as simple as opening a sandwich stand or a bicycle shop), encapsulating the concepts of the Slingshot Framework. Part of the attendance fee paid by each participant is then used as seed capital for that start-up business. This accomplishes several things simultaneously: It gives participants an immediate real-life scenario to apply the concepts to for deeper learning. It also provides local entrepreneurs with access to capital and high-level executive expertise, thus helping to boost the local economy. It fosters cross-cultural integration, as the small groups of participants become de facto board members for each local start-up business, giving them a reason to maintain regular contact. Consider the cross-cultural impact of a couple of Fortune 100 CEOs periodically advising a Central American entrepreneur on how to grow his small start-up enterprise. Everyone wins.

Sessions vary in content, complexity, and length (from half-day to multiday). To foster more personal interaction, the number of participants is limited. When the group is composed of participants who don't know one another, one up-front rule is that they are not allowed to reveal their profession, company, or title to the other participants. Rather, they are asked to interact on a first-name basis only. This simple request takes participants out of their comfort zone right from the start and allows them to bypass traditional yet shallow forms of interaction. Instead of relying on preconceived views of personality based on industry and position, it encourages participants to engage with each other freely.

The continuous relevance of IEE is based on the growing demand for meaningful executive learning, adventure travel, and deeply motivational experiences. IEE combines all three into one package.

Are Consumers Being Infatuated?

IEE is designed to create one-of-a-kind, unforgettable experiences with deep takeaway content. All ingredients for infatuating are present.

Does the Offering Create Lifestyle Enrichment?

With the rapid advance and convergence of the world around us, business leaders have less and less time at their disposal. They need to make tough choices and set priorities for what they can and cannot fit into their schedule. At the same time, they have a salient appetite for continuous learning and invigorating adventures as well as interacting with their peers. Because IEE combines these elements, they don't need to sacrifice one in favor of the other, but can enjoy them together. This provides enrichment.

Does It Overstep Traditional Boundaries and Challenge Conventional Wisdom in a Way That Is Market Driving?

IEE defies the prevailing wisdom that separates content and environment at executive learning events. In addition, the view that executives must make trade-offs between time spent on learning and having fun is made obsolete, with market-driving implications.

Does the Accordion Chart Reveal That the Offering Achieves a Broader, More Encompassing Consumer Utility?

While IEE is fundamentally an executive learning forum, the Accordion Chart process brings into focus how it is elevated to a much broader utility. IEE delivers an immersive experience that inspires self-improvement and stimulates participants' thinking in multiple directions, from business strategy to creativity, personal motivation, cultural awareness, and social responsibility.

Does the Offering Embody Value Innovation as defined by Blue Ocean Strategy?

Based on insights from the Accordion Chart process, IEE is compared to two types of alternative offerings to showcase its distinctive strategy: business conference (facility-based) and adventure travel. These are shown on the strategy canvas below. The value curves depict that while the former offers the best technical parameters (State-Of-The-Art Facility, High-Tech

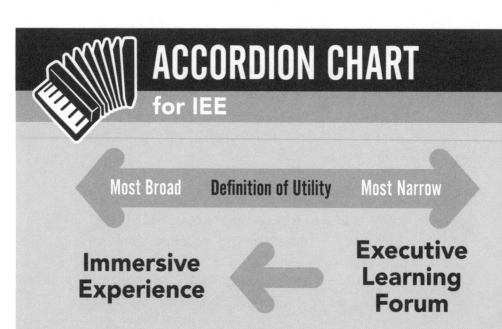

The Strategy Canvas of IEE

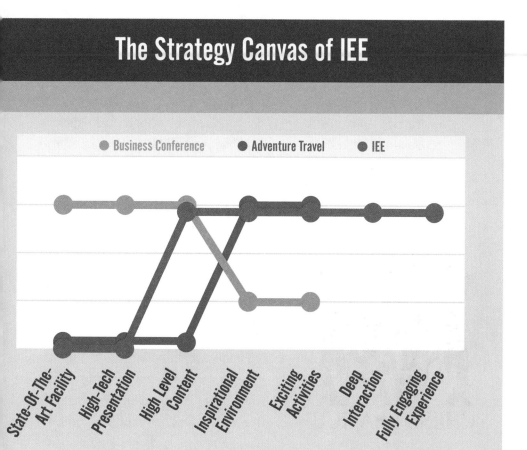

Business Conference   Adventure Travel   IEE

State-Of-The-Art Facility · High-Tech Presentation · High Level Content · Inspirational Environment · Exciting Activities · Deep Interaction · Fully Engaging Experience

Presentation format), it lacks a rousing environment and thrilling activities. In contrast, adventure travel is all about Inspirational Environment and Exciting Activities. IEE takes the best of both (High-Level Intellectual Content from conferences and Inspirational Environment and Exciting Activities from adventure travel) while eliminating the costly factors of State-Of-The-Art Facility and High-Tech Presentation format. As the environment becomes the classroom, these become unnecessary and irrelevant, and hence the source of cost savings. Their exclusion also expands the breadth of possible venues almost without limit. Lastly, IEE offers two new dimensions—Deep Interaction and Fully Engaging Experience—which complete its differentiation.

Our final example takes us back to the notion of reigniting our childhood creativity. It should come as no surprise that I set out to develop a business concept that not only exemplifies all the ideas laid out in this book but also aims to facilitate a reconnection between childhood and adulthood.

And so Team-O Entertainment was born.

Team-O is a worldwide entertainment platform focused on inventing and competing in logic-defying sports such as underwater skiing, urban sponge war, no-touch sumo wrestling, extreme bunny hop, or full-contact tubing. The *O* stands for oxymoronic, a wonderful word meaning to put together components that appear to be incompatible. From a sporting perspective, the mission of Team-O is to shift the definition of extreme sports from dangerous, highly skill-driven, and exclusive to oxymoronic, humorous, and edgy. In other words, we want *extreme* to take on the meaning of anything that is seemingly illogical and counterintuitive, yet doable by all.

Such a shift empowers ordinary people to be part of a sports pioneering movement, which can spark mass appeal for the continuous creation, playing, and viewing of oxymoronic sports. It implies that no one needs to be confined by the rules and limitations of current sports, but they can make up their own, which is actually how our most popular sports today were once invented. Think back to the stories about rugby and basketball in chapter 3. But Team-O does something even more empowering. Inventing

and playing oxymoronic sports is exactly what we all did as children, making use of random props and surroundings to fabricate
our own games. Therefore, what Team-O provides is a platform
to reconnect us with our childhood essence of limitless adventure
and to stay connected to it.

As you are reading about Team-O, perhaps you are remembering back to an invented sport from your childhood that
would be fun to resurrect. Or maybe you feel inspired to think
up a new Team-O sport by combining seemingly incompatible
components. Here are the only
criteria: the resulting sport has to
be oxymoronic, non-skill driven,
humorous, social, and make use of
ordinary props in a new way rather
than employing any elaborate
equipment. What Team-O sport
can you come up with? The world
awaits your invention.

Alongside the premise of this
book, there are numerous market
trends that point to the timeliness of Team-O. These include the
rise of extreme and whacky sports—the X-Games, the sport of
extreme ironing (look it up on Wikipedia), or the Red Bull Flugtag—
the growing popularity of adventure travel and reality television,
the proliferation of Internet- and mobile device-based social net-
works, and people's general appetite for humor, escapism, and
extraordinary experiences. In addition, there is a treasure chest
of oxymoronic sports already being cultivated by cultures around
the world, all of which can be collected and exposed. Eventually,
Team-O looks to evolve to be a new kind of International Olympic
Committee, overseeing and uniting the worldwide pursuit of oxymoronic sports, both existing and newly created.

But there's more. Remarkably scant, nevertheless persistent evidence points to the existence of a secret society with ancient and mysterious roots known as the Federation of Oxymoronic Sports (who apparently called themselves Team-O). This cultish federation seems to reach far back, perhaps to ancient times. Its members were united in a common pursuit of unconventional sports and of unconventional thinking in general, and the federation is rumored to have exerted considerable influence on the course of history from behind the scenes. Many famous, progressive thinkers of the past might have been members, but always under the veil of deep secrecy. There are fragmented indications that the federation is still intact, with the clandestine involvement of leading visionaries from around the world. No one really knows for sure. Therefore, Team-O Entertainment was named after and is dedicated to propagating the thrilling essence of the federation.

Take a look at the various components of Team-O described so far. What do you see? I see a convergence of traditionally separate entertainment channels melting into a single common platform. What is being created here is a form of all-immersive entertainment, a central repository from which consumers can receive almost any kind of entertainment they seek. Be it active or sedentary, outdoors or indoors, social or solitary, humorous or engrossing, consumers can be completely enveloped by Team-O as their primary source of entertainment content. From a business perspective, the allure is that Team-O community members will create the content for themselves; we just need to enable and manage the process. Let's take a look at these interlinking components:

1 Experimentation and Adventure. Team-O motivates people to put their imagination to the test and to formulate nonexisting sports as though they were children again. This can happen anywhere, anytime, in groups or solo. Moreover, people are inspired to seek out and expose existing oxymoronic sports.

2 Competitions. Once a sport is invented or uncovered, it sparks community playing and competition. Spontaneous competitions as well as organized, high-profile regional and international events are planned, such as the Team-O World Quest, a cross between the Olympics and the X-Games, except humorous, inclusive, and fun driven.

3 Rich Video Content. The Team-O community creates a continuous stream of content showing newly invented sports in action as well as footage of existing oxymoronic sports from around the world. Such content is entertaining to watch on any communication platform, be it in short snippets on a handheld device or on a larger screen as a new type of reality television show.

4 Multiplatform Games. The topic of Team-O is ripe for a variety of engaging games, such as contests for inventing the highest-rated new sports, finding the craziest existing sport, guessing the identity of celebrities involved with Team-O, treasure hunts for Team-O-related paraphernalia, or challenges to join various Team-O clubs.

5 **Sportswear Line and Accessories.** The designs and logo of Team-O are instant conversation starters, therefore they lend themselves naturally to a branded line of apparel and accessories.

6 **Corporate Events.** Getting executives to step outside their comfort zones via playing and inventing Team-O sports is an experiential way for them to latch on to the power of unconventional thinking. Because using ordinary objects in new, seemingly counterintuitive combinations to create a fun sport is like using the current resources of a company in unprecedented ways to drive new levels of consumer value.

7 **Unraveling the Mystery.** Just as *The Da Vinci Code* captivated consumers' imaginations, the mystery surrounding the Federation of Oxymoronic Sports is poised to ignite public curiosity. People have an opportunity to help unravel the mystery, to get involved in the discovering, sharing, and interpretation of clues about the past and current state of the federation.

8 **Social Change.** Team-O can direct attention to and affect change for needy communities or areas around the world by making them the subject of new or featured Team-O sports. For example, a call for the reenactment of the Team-O sport of Galapagos Jousting could be the front for an initiative to draw attention to the fragility of the islands and the plight of the endangered animals that inhabit them.

Are Consumers Being Infatuated?

Team-O is infectious on many levels, and its complete package of entertainment tentacles puts it in a position to be consumers' most favorite brand.

Does the Offering Create Lifestyle Enrichment?

As put forth in this book, enabling consumers to reconnect with their childhood is both liberating and empowering. Therefore Team-O is in a position to ignite lifestyle enrichment.

Does It Overstep Traditional Boundaries and Challenge Conventional Wisdom in a Way That Is Market Driving?

The all-immersive entertainment proposition of Team-O is market driving. There are strong indications that traditionally fragmented entertainment channels are converging rapidly. As one example, the ABC network created an online scavenger hunt to deepen the plot of its trippy television drama *Lost* for its hardcore followers so that the story featured in the shows could be woven further via the Internet. But Team-O takes convergence to a whole new level.

Does the Accordion Chart Reveal That the Offering Achieves a Broader, More Encompassing Consumer Utility?

Believe it or not, Team-O started out as a T-shirt design idea. Originally, the goal was to make a really cool, funny T-shirt that would be an instant conversation starter. Then, with the help of the Accordion Chart, the core utility of branded apparel was gradually expanded to arrive at the most general utility of all-immersive entertainment, and all the other components of the concept fell into place. An additional dimension of its expanded utility is that Team-O creates cross-generational entertainment, giving it a very wide target audience. There is a parallel here to the Wii, which stretched the appeal of video games across the age spectrum of the population.

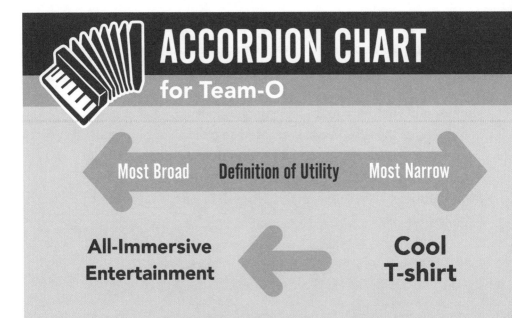

Team-O's Strategy Canvas for sports fans

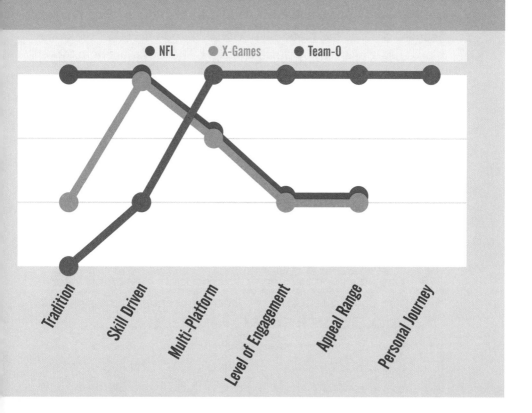

● NFL   ● X-Games   ● Team-O

Tradition · Skill Driven · Multi-Platform · Level of Engagement · Appeal Range · Personal Journey

Does the Offering Embody Value Innovation as Defined by Blue Ocean Strategy?

This is an interesting question in this case because Team-O has so many interlocking components. As a result, we have multiple options of market spaces to map via a strategy canvas. Think about Cirque du Soleil and constructing a strategy canvas to compare it against traditional circus companies. We could just as easily consider a strategy canvas for theater or opera or ballet and look at Cirque du Soleil against key players in those market segments, because the company's offering borrows elements from each.

Similarly with Team-O. We could examine Team-O's positioning on separate strategy canvases for each of the entertainment
components listed on the previous page. The strategy canvas
depicts the market space for sports, that is to say it compares
Team-O against the National Football League and the X-Games
as providers of sporting entertainment to sports fans. But remember that in such cases it's helpful to draw up a strategy canvas for
each related market space and to look for insights across them.

Take a look at the canvas. With numerous examples at your
back, answer the question yourself. Do you see evidence of Value
Innovation?

You are now in possession of a full bouquet of examples, each
illustrative of the interlocking concepts presented in the previous
chapters yet applied in a broad variety of settings. Together we
have gone full circle. We started with the premise that our childhood creativity is our personal reservoir for unconventional thinking, and we ended with an exposé of a business platform built
around reigniting that youthful sense of ingenuity.

In this book I targeted two principal drivers of successful strategy making. While the accelerated pace of change and profuse
environmental uncertainty necessitate innovation and new ways
of doing business, most people are held back by a perceived
incapacity for creative thinking and a lack of a systematic way to
harness its power. In debunking the first obstacle, my assertion
was that creative thinking is intrinsic to everyone, therefore all you
have to do is reconnect with your childhood mind-set. I then went
on to present a progressive framework to guide your continuous
application of creative thinking to build meaningful strategies.

Finally, I rested my case by sharing with you a wide assortment of real-life examples.

As adults, we have a great advantage. We have accumulated years of valuable experience and knowledge. Our challenge is not to allow such experience to cover up our childhood essence, but rather to allow them to coexist, to continuously strengthen and stimulate one another.

My approach in writing *Slingshot* was to be both forthright and concise and to rouse you to think about each point further, filling in your own examples and observations along the way, spurred on by those that I provided. After all, I did not set out to write the most sizable book, just the most infatuating and enduringly relevant.

> **"Perfection is not when there is no more
> to add, but no more to take away."**
> —Antoine de Saint-Exupéry

Echoing this sentiment from Saint-Exupéry, I am encouraged to think that you didn't find anything superfluous in what you have read and will have plenty of feedback to offer. Your feedback can then form the basis for ongoing discussions and exchanges of ideas shared by inventive adults and children alike via www.slingshotliving.com.

As you turn the page, a parting morsel of inspiration awaits you.

The slingshot of your childhood has been uncovered.

It is now up to you to grab hold and launch it again.

How will YOU reclaim YOUR childhood creativity

to defy conventional wisdom and let loose successful

strategies for your business and your life?

APPENDIX A: RADICAL IDEAS

The concepts below target a couple of major, current issues concerning American society that I think are trapped within outdated assumptions. The concepts are admittedly radical and raw. They are not meant to be fully developed nor fully feasible in their present form. Rather, they are meant to stimulate your thinking on these topics and to take you beyond conventional boundaries in search of a fresh approach. So, in a sense, they are starting platforms, or the first test launch of a slingshot.

Rethinking Higher Education

As a graduate of Amherst College and INSEAD, I can certainly appreciate the value of top-tier education. At the same time, my professional focus on helping organizations defy conventional wisdom and create their own Blue Ocean market space has led me to ponder the most relevant future format and utility of higher education. As a way of provoking discussion, I have crafted a market-driving alternative model. What follows is a quick synopsis.

Given the astounding tuition cost at leading U.S. universities (approximately $35,000 per student per year at Ivy League colleges in 2009–10), education has to be regarded as a business proposition by both students and the schools themselves. Students make an investment to attend in the hope of qualifying for well-paying jobs after graduation, while universities count on continuous donations from alumni to keep themselves going. Embracing this simple equation is the first step in universities shedding the false sanctity of outdated traditions in favor of asking such timely questions as: How can we create a model that minimizes the costs and maximizes the return for both students and universities simultaneously? How can we best enrich the lifestyles of our students in a way that they are not saddled with burdensome debt as soon as they graduate? How can we become market driving rather than simply market driven in order to attract the greatest pool of talented students? These are bold questions, indeed.

Here is a possible solution. Leading universities have amassed billions of dollars in endowment. Rather than trying to outcompete each other in endowment ratios and levels, let's tap the returns these funds generate as the basis of the new model. Let's use a portion of the endowment's yearly investment income to do away with tuition fees altogether and offer free attendance to all students. In return, once students graduate, they would contribute a percentage of their annual earnings to the school for a set number of years, or until a specified threshold is reached.

For universities with suitable resources, the cost of this program could be relatively low. For example, an annual 5 percent of the total endowment value could more than cover the full tuition of all students, meaning that colleges would only have to invest a portion of their yearly investment income, and not principal. To illustrate, here is the rough calculation for Amherst College, with rounded figures as of 2008: 5 percent of its $1.7 billion endowment would yield $50,000 for each of its 1,700 students per year, which is more than sufficient to cover current tuition. The returns would be tantalizing. Universities could select students purely on future potential from an expanded talent pool and receive far greater levels of alumni contributions than they do currently (they could even account for a portion of students not pursuing commercial careers with their degrees). For students, this model would eliminate the biggest burden of higher education altogether, that of being saddled with suffocating debt. It would also better prepare them for the postgraduation marketplace, as universities would be more motivated to offer pragmatic learning, and it would liberate them to take charge of their future with much greater flexibility. In short, there would be a close alignment of interests between students and universities.

Expanding further on the need for change, student debt programs today appear to be more and more unsustainable. According to the *Wall Street Journal*'s analysis, currently 12 percent of students default on their school loans within three years of starting repayment. Excerpts from a *Wall Street Journal* in February 2010 highlight the plight of a forty-one-year-old medical practitioner in Ohio whose student loan ballooned to over half a million dollars:

> As tuitions rise, many people are borrowing heavily to pay their bills. Some no doubt view it as "good debt," because an education can lead to a higher salary. But in practice, student loans are one of the most toxic debts, requiring extreme consumer caution....
>
> There is an estimated $730 billion in outstanding federal and private student-loan debt, says Mark Kantrowitz of FinAid.org, a website that tracks financial-aid issues—and only 40% of that debt is actively being repaid. The rest is in default, or in deferment....
>
> Dr. [Michelle] Bisutti told her 17-year-old niece the story of her debt as a cautionary tale "so the next generation of kids who want to get a higher education knows what they're getting into," she says. "I will likely have to deal with this debt for the rest of my life."

With such compelling environmental justifications, are there any visionary colleges out there willing to make the leap? Universities are often shackled by tradition and the fear of unchartered waters, even though the relevance of the way they educate is increasingly questionable. I am reminded of the old joke about psychologists: How many psychologists does it take to change a light bulb? Answer: Just one, but the bulb itself really has to want to change. Thus it is with universities, which must bravely and proactively look to reinvent themselves. With the impact and breadth of alternative education on the rise, it is just a matter of time for true pioneers to emerge.

There are already some promising signs in the direction I suggest. Several of the most prestigious and endowment-rich universities have begun offering free tuition for undergraduates from low-income families. Berea College in rural Kentucky has dropped tuition altogether for all its students. Berea offers free tuition that is funded by its endowment, donations, and by students working at least ten hours a week on campus. The results? The *New York Times* reports:

> Berea's statistics speak worlds about the demand
> for affordable higher education; this year, the col-
> lege accepted only 22 percent of its applicants.
> Among those accepted, 85 percent attended Berea,
> a yield higher than Harvard's. "You can literally come
> to Berea with nothing but what you can carry, and
> graduate debt free," said Joseph P. Bagnoli Jr., the
> associate provost for enrollment management. "We
> call it the best education money can't buy."

But even these intrepid colleges are only focused on easing or eliminating student debt burdens, which is highly commendable, but representative of only half of the formula that I am proposing. The other half—that of systematically linking alumni contributions to the future financial success of graduates—is yet to be embraced. Is there a college bold enough to try the full combination?

Rethinking the Homeless and the Elderly: The Lifeline Concept

Two of the hardest hit causalities of American society are the homeless and the solitary elderly. The Lifeline concept aims to help both simultaneously, or to be more exact, to enable them to help each other. In a nutshell, it takes homeless people off the street, gives them proper training, and sends them out to care for the elderly.

Our population is aging, and more and more elderly Americans are spending longer and longer periods alone, after their spouses pass away. Eventually, they have to take the tragically difficult step of moving into a retirement home when they are no longer able to take care of themselves, and their children are too busy to care for them.

For the most part, retirement homes are expensive and depressing, serving essentially as a waiting station for death. Many elderly experience a rapid decline after admittance, mostly because psychologically they are getting ready to pass away. Importantly, many elderly who are slated for retirement home residency don't need advanced medical care; they require only simple, consistent looking after. This presents a window of opportunity.

In parallel, a large proportion of our homeless population is not mentally ill nor addicted to drugs, but consists simply of people who have been dealt a tough hand and lost their grip on life. Instead of sinking into further and further despair and hopelessness, they could again become fully capable members of society if given a sense of purpose, usefulness, and integrity. A good illustration is the inspirational story of Chris Gardner, about whom the movie *The Pursuit of Happyness* was released in 2006, starring Will Smith. Chris and his young son, through a chain of unfortunate circumstances, were forced to be homeless before his remarkable persistence landed him an internship at a prestigious stock brokerage firm, from which he went on to become a millionaire. Lifeline targets this type of reintegration opportunity.

Concept Rollout

1 Lifeline should first be tested and perfected in a pilot project involving a suitable city and community.

2 In partnership with local organizations that work with the homeless and solitary elderly (such as shelters, churches, YMCA, etc.) potential candidates would be identified, both for caretakers and those to be looked after.

3 Qualified caretaker candidates would receive varying levels of training. The basic level would be to provide companionship and perform simple household chores (shopping, cleaning, cooking) for the elderly who have no outlet for human interaction and can no longer run their own households. The second level would involve qualification for simple, preventive medical procedures, such as administering medicine, monitoring medical conditions, etc. A third level could qualify participants for more intensive healthcare assistance.

4 In exchange, these care providers would receive a salary and benefits that would enable them to get back on their feet, find a place to live, start on a new career path; in short to begin their lives again.

Potential Benefits

1 The Lifeline concept has potential both as a driver of social change and as a successful business.

2 Here are some very rough calculations. Let's suppose conservatively that the cost of full-time residency at a senior citizen facility is $6,000 per month per person. According to MassMutual, in 2006 the national average cost for annual nursing home care was already above $75,000, which is $6,250 per month. This cost is absorbed by the elderly themselves, family members, Medicare, and insurance companies.

3 Now assuming that the qualified elderly could continue to live at their homes if they had the minimal level of care outlined above, and that a basic or midlevel Lifeline caretaker could look after three elderly people daily, then each caretaker's work would substitute approximately $18,000 per month in cost to society. This amount could more than cover the caretaker's salary and benefits, the program's training and operational expenses, and profit generation.

4 On the societal impact side, we tackle two festering problems simultaneously: we provide renewed meaning, dignity, and skills to people who are labeled as outcasts (the homeless), and we generate renewed meaning, dignity, and companionship to people labeled as helpless (the elderly).

APPENDIX B: PLAYFUL HABITS FOR GROWN-UPS

Eight Ways to Reclaim Our Childhood Creativity

By Glen Stansberry,
Creator of lifedev.net

Growing up, I didn't play with a whole lot of store-bought toys. It's not that my parents didn't provide enough tools to stimulate my young mind. In fact, it was quite the opposite: my parents had given me the best toy a young boy could have. I was raised in the country.

Living in the middle of nowhere for the first part of my childhood meant that I didn't need very many toys to keep me happy. Instead I preferred activities such as climbing trees, turning hay bales into forts, and tromping through the woods, to name a few. I learned quickly that the best fun was the kind made with your own imagination.

When Did We Outgrow "Imagination"?

How many times as children did we take mundane materials like sheets and couch cushions to create castles and forts? I distinctly remember using a toilet plunger as a sword many a time in the early years. (What?! It seemed like a good idea at the time…) For some reason as adults we "grow" out of this creative mindset and started worrying about the everyday bits of life. While this is important for functioning in society, it sure puts a damper on being creative.

Kids are some of the best problem solvers around. Give a kid motivation for solving a problem, and he'll use whatever resources are handy to get it done. Not only that, he won't quit until he's found the solution. Kids have the perfect blend of determination, creativity, and downright recklessness to find a solution.

So where did adults go wrong? I'd argue that we stopped listening to the inner child and started listening to our bosses, or worse, our insecurities. Now we see the world through jaded eyes, and what was once wonderful is now commonplace. But it doesn't have to be like that. Here are a few ways to recapture that mind-set of a creative child:

1 **Eliminate pesky technology distractions.** How many small children do you know that check their e-mail constantly? Or are constantly on the phone? Yeah, me neither.

2 **Stop multitasking.** Kids have a one-track mind. Unlike the awful training that they'll receive when they're older, at a young age they have the incredible ability to not only focus on the task at hand, but to *fixate* on it.

3 **Seek alone time.** It never ceases to amaze me how productive kids are when they're playing by themselves. They are literally the masters of getting into the flow.

4 **Be silly.** I'm not joking. While this is what kids are notorious for, it can actually be an incredible tactic to really think outside the box. How many major breakthroughs and products were developed around some guy having a lazy beer with another friend, posing unlikely "what if" scenarios. For example:

> *Bill Hewlett: (Chuckling) "Hey Dave, what if someone made a computer that was smaller than a room, and people could use them in their homes?! Oh man, that would be crazy rad. David Packard: "Hrm…"*

Being silly allows you to explore those scenarios that you wouldn't bother with if you were thinking like a responsible adult.

5 **Nap times.** Unfortunately, as we've gotten older we tend to overlook the fact that growing up, we had nap times at the *same time every day*. While we may not need a daily afternoon siesta, the principle still remains: make sure rest is a priority. Rest is essential for creativity, and without it we don't leave enough resources to think outside the box. We're more interested in getting through the day.

6 **Milk and cookies.** Ahh yes…who doesn't love milk and cookies? Milk and cookies stand for the simple pleasures that we overlook every day because we're too busy. Simple treats in our day can make a huge difference in our overall attitude and boost our mood. Have you ever had a splurge of creativity while being depressed? It's hard to be creative while grumpy. Have a cookie.

7 **Test the boundaries.** Anyone who's spent more than five minutes with a two-year-old knows what this means. Kids will always, *always* try to push the limits. While this can be pretty frustrating as a parent, it can be a good thing as a child. Without testing boundaries, the child doesn't learn what he can't do, or more importantly, what he *can* do. As adults, we can easily become complacent. But true innovation means that we have to be willing to take risks and test the boundaries. Tim Ferriss puts it best by saying we should implement first and apologize later (only if it blows up).

8 **See the world with wonder.** Einstein was famous for this. Because his language developed slowly as a lad, it allowed him to look in wonder at the common things most people don't take a second look at. "The ordinary adult never bothers his

head about the problems of space and time." These are things he has thought of as a child. "Consequently, I probed more deeply into the problem than an ordinary child would have." Einstein's ability to see the world with a child's eyes gave him a unique insight on everyday findings, which eventually led to some of the world's most amazing breakthroughs in science.

Slingshot "Imagination Kit" Challenge

The purpose of the challenge is to enable participants to re-ignite their sense of limitless exploration, imagination, and resourcefulness that they had as children.

The challenge is very simple. Participants form small teams of no more than six members. Each team is given an Imagination Kit. The challenge for the teams is to come up with the most fun game using only the content of the kit within a short time limit (e.g. 30 minutes). Teams must also come up with catchy names for their new games.

The kit contains an eclectic mix of everyday items which participants are asked to view as components of a game. Therefore the challenge alters their perspective and broadens their mental boundaries of what is possible—just as children do all the time. Teams are free to use as few or as many of the items as they want, and to utilize their surroundings as part of the game (e.g. tables, chairs, walls, etc).

All participants can cast votes for their favorite game as a way of determining the winners (but no one can vote for their own), or an external panel can act as judges (it is often fun and effective to include children in the panel). A subsequent Slingshot Challenge Day can be organized where the teams compete against each other on each of the top 10 new games.

Slingshot Imagination Kit—sample content:

1. small roll of duck tape, e.g. 10 yards (10m) in length
2. 6 decorator balloons
3. 12 wooden clothespins
4. 1 daily newspaper
5. 6 plastic party cups
6. thin rope, 20–30 feet (5–10m) in length
7. 2 wooden yardsticks or wooden rulers
8. small bag of uncooked rice or beans

The World's Best-Selling Toy

What do you think takes the title as the world's most popular toy? It is none other than the Rubik's Cube. By some estimates more than a billion people have come in contact with one. Its popularity goes unabated almost forty years since its creation in 1974 by Hungarian sculptor and professor of architecture Ernö Rubik and stretches well beyond the realm of toys.

The cube is a fascinating puzzle, a majestic piece of art, and a cultural icon. It spurs ongoing discussion forums and world-wide competitions. The highly coveted, reigning world record for solving the cube is less than seven seconds. The cube appears on permanent exhibit in New York's Museum of Modern Art, has its own agent in Hollywood, and is cited in the *Oxford English Dictionary*. It appeals incomparably to children and adults alike, all across the globe. Have you picked one up lately?

RESOURCES

Andrews, Steve. "Polk Undercover Drug Investigators Play Wii During Raid." News Channel 8, Tampa, FL, September 21, 2009, www2.tbo.com/content/2009/sep/21/undercover-drug-investigators-embarrass-polk-sheri/.

Bagnato, Andrew. "Texas Tech 44, Minnesota 41." Rivals.com, December 30, 2006, rivals.yahoo.com/ncaa/football/recap?gid=200612290031&prov=ap.

Bird, Cameron. "Found: Amusement Park Ride From the Future." *Wired,* November 17, 2009, www.wired.com/magazine/2009/11/found_amusement_park_ride/3/.

Byron, Ellen. "Razor Burn: A Flood of Fancy Shavers Leaves Some Men Feeling Nicked." *Wall Street Journal,* July 12, 2010, http://online.wsj.com/article/SB10001424052748704699604575343210255777650.html.

Clark, Aaron. "What's Up in the Air?" *Travel and Leisure Magazine,* January 2007, www.travelandleisure.com/articles/global-warming-and-the-travelers-world.

"Coke v Pepsi: Things Go Worse with Coke." *Economist,* December 14, 2005, www.economist.com/node/5308326.

"Cool Things You Can Design Yourself." *Bloomberg Businessweek,* April 10, 2010.

Deutschman, Alan. "The Fabric of Creativity." Fast Company Magazine, December 1, 2004. www.fastcompany.com/magazine/89/open_gore.html.

"Excursion to Pompeii and Herculaneum." Romecarservice.it, www.romecarservice.it/pompeii-herculanum.htm.

Gallo, Carmine. "Lessons in Simplicity from the Flip." *Bloomberg Businessweek,* February 17, 2010, http://www.businessweek.com/smallbiz/content/feb2010/sb20100217_244373.htm.

Hawe, Jim. "A New Style: QB Net Had an Idea: Fast, Cheap Haircuts." *Wall Street Journal,* September 22, 2003.

Hechiner, John, and Tom McGinty. "For-Profit Schools See More Defaults." *Wall Street Journal,* December 14, 2009, http://online.wsj.com/article/SB126075983194590097.html.

Jana, Reena. "Recession: The Mother of Innovation?" *Bloomberg Businessweek,* July 22, 2009, www.businessweek.com/innovate/content/jul2009/id20090722_943951.htm.

Johnson, Mark W. "Amazon's Smart Innovation Strategy." *Bloomberg Businessweek,* April 12, 2010, www.businessweek.com/innovate/content/apr2010/id20100412_520351.htm.

Lewin, Tamar. "With No Frills or Tuition, a College Draws Notice." *New York Times,* July 21, 2008, www.nytimes.com/2008/07/21/education/21endowments.html?_r=1&pagewanted=1.

"The Little Car." In *We See.* Read with Dick and Jane, no. 9. New York: Grosset & Dunlap, 2004.

"Man United Boss Declares Club Is the Richest in the World." Daily Mail, January 11, 2008, www.dailymail.co.uk/news/article-507567/Man-United-boss-declares-club-richest-world.html.

Martin, Susan Taylor. "Steve Forbes, Eckerd College Professor John Prevas Look to Caesar for Leadership Lessons." *St. Petersburg Times,* May 24, 2009, www.tampabay.com/news/perspective/article1003209.ece.

Morris, Betsy. "The New Rules." *Fortune,* August 2, 2006, money.cnn.com/magazines/fortune/fortune_archive/2006/07/24/8381625/index.htm.

Nadler, John. "Blue Ocean Strategy." *Business Hungary,* October 2005, amcham.nextra.hu/BUSINESSHUNGARY/19-10/articles/08-feature-01.asp.

Naughton, Keith. "Small: It's the New Big." *Newsweek,* February 16, 2008, www.newsweek.com/2008/02/16/small-it-s-the-new-big.html.

Norris, Michele. "'Hand-and-Run' Artist Strikes NYC Museums." NPR, March 24, 2005, www.npr.org/templates/story/story.php?storyId=4559961.

Pilon, Mary. "The $555,000 Student-Loan Burden." *Wall Street Journal,* February 16, 2010, http://online.wsj.com/article/SB10001424052748703389004575033063806327030.html.

Pogue, David. "Camcorder Brings Zen to the Shoot." *New York Times,* March 20, 2008, www.nytimes.com/2008/03/20/technology/personaltech/20pogue.html.

Schmid, Randolph E. "Raising Prices Enhances Wine Sales." *USA Today*, January 14, 2008, www.usatoday.com/money/economy/2008-01-14-3797024451_x.htm.

Schubert, Siri. "Taking Robots for a Ride." CNN Money, August 1, 2005, money.cnn.com/magazines/business2/business2_archive/2005/08/01/8269666/index.htm.

Schwartz, Ariel. "Swirl Turns Washing Clothes Into a Game." Fast Company, February 5, 2010, www.fastcompany.com/blog/ariel-schwartz/sustainability/swirl-turns-washing-clothes-game.

Storey, David, et al. "Sign of the Times: Even Cheaper Store Kills Off Cheap Store." Reuters, January 14, 2009, www.reuters.com/article/2009/01/14/us-financial-times-idUSTRE50D1B120090114.

Toppo, Greg. "See 'Dick and Jane'—Again." *USA Today*, February 25, 2004, www.usatoday.com/life/books/news/2004-02-25-dick-and-jane-main_x.htm.

"12 Things That Became Obsolete This Decade." Huffington Post, December 15, 2009, www.huffingtonpost.com/2009/12/26/obsolete-things-that-expi_n_402674.html.

Van Itallie, Nancy. *Fodor's Florence, Tuscany, and Umbria*. New York: Fodor's, 1993.

"Where a Cell Phone Is Still Cutting Edge." *New York Times*, April 9, 2010.

Wortham, Jenna. "Cellphones Now Used More for Data than for Calls" *New York Times*, May 14, 2010, www.nytimes.com/2010/05/14/technology/personaltech/14talk.html.

INDEX

ABOUT THE AUTHOR

Gabor **George Burt** was born in Budapest, Hungary. He holds a BA in psychology from Amherst College as well as an MBA from INSEAD, France.

Over the past decade Gabor has gained international recognition in the management world as a pioneer in the strategic perspective of Defying Conventional Wisdom, as well as a leading expert on Blue Ocean Strategy, the influential framework that transforms unconventional ideas into successful strategies. He is actively involved in shaping strategy for a diverse group of international clients from Fortune 500 firms to successful start-ups and leading by example through his own initiatives, such as the Immersive Executive Experience series and Team-O Entertainment.

Gabor writes articles for leading business publications and co-hosts a nationally broadcast radio show. His blog has been selected as one of the top online resources on innovation. Gabor has been featured in the book *Radical Action for Radical Times*, contributed case study material for the record-breaking book *Blue Ocean Strategy*, and is the author of the upcoming *Appetizers of Wit and Wisdom*, a collection of comic anecdotes and provocative observations.

Inspiration for this book came from Gabor's wide-ranging experience as a strategist, business developer, idea liberator, and provocateur, from his fun-loving wife and four incomparable children.